Teachers
Teaching
Teachers

Thank you
for making a
Difference!

enjoy

André Castelli

eXtreme teaching
rigorous texts for troubled times

Joe L. Kincheloe and Danny Weil
General Editors

Vol. 8

PETER LANG
New York • Washington, D.C./Baltimore • Bern
Frankfurt am Main • Berlin • Brussels • Vienna • Oxford

Geneal G. Cantrell & Gregory L. Cantrell

Teachers
Teaching
Teachers

Wit, Wisdom, and Whimsey for Troubled Times

PETER LANG
New York • Washington, D.C./Baltimore • Bern
Frankfurt am Main • Berlin • Brussels • Vienna • Oxford

Library of Congress Cataloging-in-Publication Data

Cantrell, Geneal G.
Teachers teaching teachers: wit, wisdom, and whimsey
for troubled times / Geneal G. Cantrell, Gregory L. Cantrell.
p. cm. — (Extreme teaching: rigorous texts for troubled times; v. 8)
Includes bibliographical references.
1. Teaching. 2. Teachers. I. Cantrell, Gregory L. II. Title. III. Series.
LB1025.3 .C38   371.1—dc21   2002028268
ISBN 0-8204-6303-5
ISSN 1534-2808

Die Deutsche Bibliothek-CIP-Einheitsaufnahme

Cantrell, Geneal G.:
Teachers teaching teachers: wit, wisdom, and whimsey
for troubled times / Geneal G. Cantrell; Gregory L. Cantrell.
–New York; Washington, D.C./Baltimore; Bern;
Frankfurt am Main; Berlin; Brussels; Vienna; Oxford: Lang.
(Extreme teaching; Vol. 8)
ISBN 0-8204-6303-5

Cover design by Joni Holst

The paper in this book meets the guidelines for permanence and durability
of the Committee on Production Guidelines for Book Longevity
of the Council of Library Resources.

© 2003 Peter Lang Publishing, Inc., New York
275 Seventh Avenue, 28th Floor, New York, NY 10001
www.peterlangusa.com

Printed in the United States of America

This book is dedicated to all of the teachers who work each day to light the "fire" of the love of learning in all of their students and to those who aspire to follow in that rich tradition. We especially recognize all of the teachers who kindled that fire for us.

TABLE OF CONTENTS

FOREWORD

Year after year an eager crop of new teachers arrives at the doors of our nation's schools. Many are fresh out of their teacher preparation programs. For the most part, they are excited and enthusiastic, and possess the feeling of being able to conquer the world to motivate, inspire, and teach students in their charge. These teachers enter the profession (as we did) to make a difference in the lives of children. It is exciting to see these young novice teachers, yet frustrating to watch as they face the stark realities of today's ever-challenging classrooms. What has happened to our schools? What does the system need to do to better prepare these novice teachers for the "trench warfare" that is all too often occurring in the classroom?

This work will focus on some basic guiding principles that can serve as a compass to give direction, sustain, and renew educators in their journey toward educating the students in our charge. These principles are based on those characteristics and behaviors that are observed in successful teachers' classrooms, and each will be addressed in a given chapter. Instructional content will *not* be discussed except in relation to the topics, which include building relationships, motivation, communication, class management, humor, stress management, professional growth, and the power of the profession.

Creating and sustaining a community of learners is paramount to the success of effective classrooms. This creating and sustaining of community permeates the proposed text. While explicit and implied theory will be embedded, the use of real-life reflections and stories about schools and classrooms will connect, illustrate, and solidify theoretical concepts presented. This approach will make an inspiring, reflective, and practical delivery system for the understanding and internalization of these *compass principles*.

Our combined background of more than 50 years of teaching and administrative experience at multiple levels, as well as having had the opportunity to grow up in the rural South, will serve as a platform to frame an experience-based approach to the problems existing in today's schools. Our passion for education, teaching, and children will be evident as the reader follows the flow of each principle demonstrated. This use of real-life experiences and reflections, which may evoke emotions ranging from tears to laughter, will serve to drive the major points the authors wish to convey to the very heart of the importance of the democratic and socially just classroom. Further, emphasis on the concept of teacher creativity will be connected to the concept of overall classroom success. This type of teaching is especially important at a time when diversity in the classroom and high-stakes testing is at an all-time high in American schools.

ACKNOWLEDGMENTS

The authors would like to thank all of the teachers and students who have both contributed to this work as well as inspired it. It is their stories that serve as the "glue" to connect the theory with the practice.

We thank Helen Stratton for her professional assistance in the technical aspects of this project as well as her friendship.

Also, we acknowledge the encouragement and support of Dr. Denise Crockett who pushed us to put pen to paper.

Finally, to Dr. Joe Kincheloe, whose wisdom, experience, and encouragement has been integral in the completion of this project.

CHAPTER 1

Kids Don't Care How Much You Know 'til They Know How Much You Care

Understanding and Building Relationships and Community in the Classroom

Recently, while working with a gathering of veteran mentor teachers, the group was participating in an activity that centered on their descriptions of attributes of teachers who were most memorable in their lives. They were describing their favorite teachers! What a wonderful scene! These veteran teachers, all now actively involved in mentoring teacher candidates, were reflecting on their educational careers and exactly what made their most memorable teachers so influential in their own lives. As the activity concluded, with the last sticky note being placed on the wreath of honor, the excitement in the room was quite evident. Each mentor had difficulty simply naming the attributes of his or her favorite teacher, stories had to be heard, and each had to give the meaning behind the attributes. As we led the group through the remainder of the exercise and categorized these attributes, a question was raised that was most interesting. It was: Before we discuss the combined list of attributes of great teachers, what issues are you spending most of your time discussing with your current mentees?

Again, this was an easy task for them to recount and spout off the areas where their teacher candidates were weak and unskilled. The list of concerns included items such as curriculum standards, lesson planning, classroom procedures, management, school regulations, schedules, bus duty, grading papers, working with parents, and so on. The interesting part of this exercise came when we asked them to compare the list generated by the mentors regarding the attributes of their most influential teachers and the list of conversation topics they discussed with their mentees. Can you predict how the two lists compared?

As it happens, the two lists were almost opposite. The attributes revered by the mentors when describing their most influential teachers were such characteristics as: accessible, believed in me, cared about me, went the extra mile for his or her students, cool, made learning fun, never gave up on me, fair, helped me to see my potential, and so on. These attributes were in the area of the affective domain. The relationship with their favorite teacher was so important to the mentor teachers that many had carried these cherished memories with them for decades. Does this disturb you? In comparison the list of what the mentors spent time discussing with their mentees was more procedural and cognitive while the list of traits of the favorite teachers accents the affective—namely, relationship and community building. Undeniably the attribute exercise asked for characteristics of teachers that influenced the mentor whereas the second list reflected realities in the mentor/mentee relationship. However shouldn't those attributes of influential teachers entail a portion of our discussions with teacher candidates? When you ask novice teachers why they entered the teaching profession, the most common response to the question is to make a difference in someone's life. It bothers the authors that we ignore these important conversations with our novice teachers. Why don't we stop and take the time to make a conscious effort to discuss the deeper meanings and values of teaching? If these are the motivators present when we entered the profession, why do we not celebrate them as we, veteran educators, work with our young teachers to perpetuate our profession? After all, isn't it the deeper meaning that will, in essence, cause us to remain in the profession? Are we trying to discover shortcuts and quick fixes for how to become a good teacher the same as we are trying to prescribe narrowly focused curriculum standards called education for our students? While an educated citizenry is imperative to economic development, have we in fact reduced schooling to a process that plays into a bigger picture, which was never the original intention of our forefathers? Just what is schooling? Is it merely an economic preparation for a vocation or is it something more? If schooling entails all that embodies lifelong learning, then schooling certainly is something more! Is teaching an art? Yes. Is teaching a science? Yes. However, teaching is not a step-by-step recipe. We must embrace the importance of these questions and we must make time to form the essential relationships not only with our mentees but, more importantly, with the very students who sit in our classrooms.

Perhaps the concept of relationship development is, in fact, the cornerstone to the foundation of successful classrooms. Have we lost sight of the power of these important relationship concepts in the current environment of high-stakes testing? As teacher candidates leave the surroundings of their own P–12 experiences and enter teacher education programs, do we assume that they, too, have had the same experiences with influential teachers as have our mentor teachers, or do we need to emphasize even more the relationship significance to a higher degree? The alternative to not doing this is to allow novice teachers to flounder, and for some to fail, as they struggle with the induction year. This chapter will deal with these questions and more.

Caring Teachers

> What happens in the classroom between people is more important than any assignment, curriculum, procedure, or content. If the people relate to each other in an environment of acceptance and trust, content and competence will grow.
>
> —Children Are People Curriculum

Most teacher candidates will say they entered the teaching profession because of a strong desire to work with young people, a love for children, and the need to make a difference. Without question, this initial commitment to the profession is critical to the effectiveness of classroom teachers. The National Commission on Teaching and America's Future (1996) set as a goal qualified, caring, competent teachers for every child by 2006. Questions and doubts as to the quality of our nation's teachers are on the rise with the ever-increasing focus on standards, accountability, and testing in our classrooms. However, the authors feel that establishing relationships with our students is undeniably at the very heart of what constitutes teaching and learning. Effective teachers understand the importance of teacher-student relationships. Students between the ages of 6 and 12 spend nearly a quarter of their waking lives with teachers (Jones & Jones, 1998). Teachers who fail to take the necessary time to establish heartfelt bonds with students often experience constant classroom disruptions; unhappy, unproductive students; and dissatisfaction with the teaching profession. In tandem, students who cannot relate to their teachers often do not show respect for their teachers. To maintain order in a classroom and to be able to teach students, a teacher must be able to establish the following essential connections: a teacher must get to know his or her students personally, socially, emotionally, and academically.

Learning requires emotional safety, caring, and respect. Students need to feel free to ask questions, participate openly and honestly in class discussions, take intellectual risks, and be a part of the bigger community. Without the support, nurturing, and care of teachers in a classroom, efforts to build a community where learning can occur is almost impossible (Lappan & Ferrini-Mundy, 1993).

A significant body of research exists that supports the effect of positive teacher-student relationships on academic achievement. Wells (1989) found that students who felt liked by their teachers had higher academic achievement than those who did not. When I have asked students in interviews what makes a particular teacher "special" and worthy of respect, the students consistently cited three characteristics: firmness; compassion; and an interesting, engaging, or challenging teaching style (Noguera, 1995). Rogers and Webb (1991) conducted a study on caring in schools and found a recurring theme: Good teachers care, and good teaching is inextricably linked to specific acts of caring.

What is caring? Is it just the creation of a warm, friendly relationship with our students? Is it going to a ball game to watch our students play? Is it sending a card to a student in the hospital? Certainly it is all of the above and much more. Caring involves talking and listening to our students, saying encouraging words and presenting supportive actions, and taking an interest in the students' lives both inside and outside the classroom. William Glasser (1990), in his book *The Quality School: Managing Students without Coercion*, wrote:

> Students tell me that a good teacher is deeply interested in the students and in the material being taught. They also say that such a teacher frequently conducts class discussions and does not lecture very much. Almost all of them say that a good teacher relates to them on their level; the teacher does not place herself above them, and they are comfortable talking to her. (p. 66)

Teachers have opportunities to establish caring in all interactions with their students. A teacher's classroom behavior is often under scrutiny by his or her students. As a result, students learn a great deal (perhaps more) from a teacher's nonverbal behaviors than his or her verbal behaviors (Galloway, 1976). A teacher's facial expression, gaze, posture, gestures, and other body movements provide the student with valuable information about his or her emotional state, attitudes toward students, and even familiarity with the lesson content. Ramsey (1979) suggests that students determine how a teacher feels about them simply by observing the teacher's communication behaviors. More on the power and effect of nonverbal communication can be found in chapter 4.

One assumption made about teacher-student relationships is that the behavior patterns of the teacher dictate, or at least affect, the behavior patterns of the students. Presumably, the more that students perceive their teacher cares about them, the more likely they will pay attention, be less disruptive, and consequently master course material. McCroskey (1992) advanced the concept of "perceived caring" as a central perception of teachers on the part of students. He suggests that it is probably best if the teacher really cares about the student, but notes that it is challenging for any teacher to care a great deal about every student especially high school teachers, who often have large classes and over 150 total students in their charge. Thus, it is important for teachers to learn how to communicate in such a way that each student perceives that the teacher cares about him or her, whether or not that is the case in reality. It is not the caring that counts; it is the perception of caring that is critical. It would be utterly foolish to insist that all teachers should care about all of their students. If you teach long enough, you will encounter a student or two who challenges your every wit and will. In the South, clichés such as "he rubs me the wrong way," "she gets on my last nerve," or "we don't see eye to eye" are good descriptors of such students. However, as the adult in this situation (and you may have to remind yourself of this point), you must not let the student get the best of you. In this case, it becomes even more critical for the students to perceive that you care about them in order for them to be successful, productive students in your classroom. Furthermore, if a teacher cares deeply about his or her students, but does not communicate that feeling, he or she might as well not care at all. An abbreviated version of a story that has made the rounds of many teacher education programs and school staff development sessions follows, to serve as an illustration of this point....

> It started with tragedy on a cold February morning. I was driving behind the school bus as I did most mornings on my way to school. It veered and stopped at the local hotel and came to an unexpected stop. A boy lurched out of the bus and stumbled on the curb. The bus driver and I reached him at the same moment.
>
> "He's dead," the driver whispered.
>
> It didn't register for a minute. I glanced at the scared young faces staring down at us from the school bus. "A doctor! Quick! I'll phone from the hotel."
>
> "No use. I tell you, he's dead." The driver looked down at the boy's still form. "He never even said he felt bad," he muttered, "just tapped me on the shoulder and said, real quiet, 'I'm sorry. I have to get off at the hotel.' That's all."
>
> At school, the usual giggling, shuffling morning noise quieted as the news went down the halls. I passed a huddle of girls. "Who was it? Who dropped dead on the way to school?," I heard one of them half whisper.
>
> "Don't know his name," was the reply.
>
> It was like that in the faculty room and the principal's office. "I'd appreciate you going out to tell the parents," the principal told me. "They don't have a phone, and anyway, somebody from school should go there in person. I'll cover your classes."
>
> "Why me?" I asked. "Wouldn't it better if you did it?"
>
> "I didn't know the boy," the principal flatly admitted. "Besides in last year's sophomore personality's column I noticed that you were listed as his favorite teacher."
>
> I got in my car and drove out to the boy's home. Me, his favorite teacher! Why, he hadn't spoken two words to me in two years! I could see him in my mind's eye all right, sitting back there in the last seat in my afternoon literature class. He came in the room by himself and left by himself. "Cliff Evans," I muttered to myself, the boy who never smiled. I never saw him smile once.
>
> The big ranch kitchen was clean and warm. I blurted out my news somehow. Mrs. Evans reached blindly for a chair. "He never said anything about not feeling good."
>
> His stepfather snorted. "He ain't said nothin' about anything since I moved in here."
>
> Mrs. Evans got up, pushed a pan to the back of the stove, and began to untie her apron. "Now hold on," her husband snapped. "I got to have breakfast before I go to town. Nothin' we can do now anyway. If Cliff hadn't been so dumb, he'd have told us he didn't feel good."

After school I sat in the office and stared bleakly at the records spread out before me. I was asked to write his obituary for the school paper. The almost bare sheets mocked the effort. "Cliff Evans, white, never legally adopted by stepfather, five half-brothers and sisters." These meager strands of information and the list of D grades were about all the records had to offer.

Cliff Evans had silently come in the school door each morning and gone out the school door each evening, and that was all. He never belonged to a club. He never played on a team. He never held an office. As far as I could tell, he had never done one happy, noisy kid thing. He had never been anybody at all.

How do you go about making a boy into a zero? The grade-school records showed me much of the answer. The first and second grade teachers' annotations read "sweet, shy child; timid but eager." Then the third grade note had opened the attack. Some teacher had written in a good, firm hand, "Cliff won't talk. Uncooperative. Slow learner." The other academic sheep had followed with "dull," "slow-witted," "low IQ." They became correct. The boy's IQ score in the ninth grade listed at 83. But his IQ in the third grade had been 106. The score didn't go under 100 until the seventh grade. Even timid, sweet children have resilience. It takes time to break them.

We recall watching a 16-millimeter film in the 1970s recounting the story of Cliff; we remember the title as *Cipher in the Snow* (Atkinson, 1973). We're not exactly sure if the account is true, but the powerful message it communicates touches the heart and has proven memorable! Certainly this seems likes an exaggerated case of not caring for our students but an important message nonetheless.

How can we communicate a sense of caring to our students? A simple way to demonstrate caring to your students is through listening. Glasser (1988) states that 95% of discipline problems that occur in schools can be attributed to no one listening to their concerns, ideas or opinions. Students need to believe that someone whom they respect will listen to them. Secondly, teachers need someone to listen and accept the validity of student's statements or concerns. Think for a minute about the last time that a student approached your desk and wanted to tell you something. It could have been that they just wanted you to notice the brand new pair of shoes dad bought them at the mall last night or maybe they were upset about something that happened at home before getting on the school bus or maybe they wanted to share a funny story. What did you do? If you are like most teachers, you half listened (grading papers or checking the roll) to the student sharing the story, while providing a small nod, and giving a quick response or suggesting a quick fix for the student's concerns. The following personal story (a reflection actually shared with first-year teachers) brings to light the significance of simply listening and showing compassion to your students.

Well it's Sunday night and I'm thinking that I should use this opportunity to shed a little light on what my mom used to call "life's little lessons." What lessons, you ask?

Please just indulge me for a minute and read on. For those of you who know me well, you know that I have a precious little dog—a beagle. Her name is Holly. She is such an integral part of our home and daily lives. Why, I even selected the book *Shiloh* to use as a model for a project in my Children's Literature class just so I could show my "students" her baby picture! I have to tell you, she is so cute!

During the night this past Friday Holly got sick but this was nothing unusual because she'd been sick a couple of times. She had a little sore spot on her tummy but with the high humidity and the heat we thought that was normal, right? However, throughout the day on Saturday she continued to be sick. We called the vet, gave him all the details, made an appointment for Monday, and gave her some Pepto Bismol to settle her stomach, per the doctor's instructions. She wasn't able to hold the medicine down, either. Later in the evening my husband noticed she was not breathing right and we proceeded to take her to the emergency animal care hospital. They immediately took her and placed her on IV; she was dehydrated and had a fever of 105 degrees. The doctor wanted to keep her through the night. I won't go into all the details on what he thought could be wrong with her, but needless to say, it was serious. He said we should call in the morning around eight o'clock. His call came before ours; I knew the news as soon as I heard the phone ring at five in the morning. Holly did not make it!

Now I know you are asking yourself why in the world would I want to share this sad tale with you? There are several reasons.

First, as a professional educator I've come to believe in the importance and the efficacy of reflective writing. Writing this is helping me. I know that in my heart we didn't do anything wrong. We did all we could.

Second, I truly believe in the importance of modeling. If I ask you to reflect on your work and grow to become a reflective practitioner, I should, too. Thanks for allowing me to share this with you.

And now on to the life lessons…

Being human, we always try to make sense of things that happen in our lives that just don't seem to add up. How can I find sense in Holly passing away? She was only five years old and the doctor still doesn't know what happened. We may never be able to answer that question, but I do know some things.

As a classroom teacher I often found myself with far too little time to listen to all the things my students wanted to share with me. A hand goes up during a class discussion. "Does this have something to do with the lesson?" I ask. "Is it a question?" "Can it wait?" Sometimes a student would make their way up to my desk while I was busy grading papers, taking attendance, filling out forms or writing lesson plans. I'd listen, of course, while continuing to go about the "business of teaching." I now think back to some of those times and question my reaction to their concerns. "Oh, I'm sorry your dog died last night, it'll be OK; now go back to your desk. We need to get busy on your seatwork!"

Ouch!

Lesson #1: Listen to your students and take their concerns to heart.

Holly (like most dogs) loved her owners unconditionally! As teachers, shouldn't we also love our students unconditionally? I know firsthand how hard that is, but isn't that why we chose to go into this profession?

Lesson #2: Never, ever give up on a student!
You may be their last best chance at making it in this crazy world. Help them to set goals and help them to believe in themselves.

Lesson #3: Life lessons…they're not always easy; learn from them. Once you've experienced them you are never really quite the same. Holly made a positive difference in my life.

I hope I'll be able to do the same with you as you complete your first year of teaching.

I know you can do that with your students!

This reflection was shared with one of Geneal's induction teacher classes. After teaching and working with induction teachers for several years, Geneal finally realized the importance of a caring community where all members are valued and respected for their contributions, even with adults! Years earlier in teaching the course she was far too busy trying to get the "curriculum" all covered, overlooking the important first step to an effective classroom—establishing a relationship with your students and building a learning community. The first days of any class should be used to get to know your students, find out their interests and hobbies, and to allow them to get to know you as well. As the reflection reveals, the importance of simply listening to students share their stories and concerns is one way that teachers can begin to build important connections with their students.

Another consideration, which focuses on building relationships in the classroom, includes the attributes of empathy, understanding, and responsiveness. These attributes, identified by McCroskey (1992), can lead students to perceive the teacher as caring about their welfare. Empathy is the capacity to see a situation from the point of view of another person and feel how they feel about it. When students see teachers behaving in positive ways toward them, it is reasonable to interpret that behavior as the teacher's concern for them. Some teachers in instructional situations are able to see things from the student's perspective, while others are unable or unwilling. When a teacher can understand a student's point of view and also respect it, the teacher may be granted more credibility, and students are more likely to believe the teacher genuinely cares about them. Phenomenologists study the view of the world from the actor's own frame of reference. For them, the importance lies in what people imagine it to be. As teachers we must learn to see the world through the lens of a child and view the world as they do (Patton, 1980). When we can successfully do this, students will begin to see their teachers as empathetic.

A second factor that leads students to perceive teachers as caring is that of understanding. Understanding is the ability to comprehend another person's feelings and needs. Perceived understandings have been found to have a positive impact in a variety of communication contexts (Cahn, 1986). Some teachers are quite good at determining when students have a problem either personally or academically, while others seem very insensitive to these things, much like in the case of Cliff Evans. Teachers who are able to communicate and understand their students may indeed have more experiences of their own that have helped them to understand human relationships. At any rate, when students observe a teacher exhibiting such behaviors, they are more likely to perceive the teacher as caring about them.

Finally, a third factor of perceived caring is responsiveness. Responsiveness occurs when teachers react to a student's needs quickly or when a teacher listens to the student's concerns or problems (McCroskey, 1992). Responsiveness has been found to be very important to the way teachers are perceived by the students (Robinson, 1995). A responsive teacher recognizes and reacts to students, while the nonresponsive teacher's behavior is not personalized to the students. A highly unresponsive teacher would be one who is a prisoner to the desk and lectures or reads notes. Conversely, an interactive responsive teacher modifies his or her behaviors throughout the class period depending on how the students are reacting to the class. They can read student's faces, interpret body language, and modify and adjust accordingly. Students who perceive a teacher regularly responding to them may also perceive the teacher as caring more about them.

A simple examination of all juncture made by the authors up until this point comes together to make one definitive statement: *Kids don't care what you know until they know you care!* Effective teachers know and practice this concept instinctively. There is a story about a man recommending a plumber to his neighbor. "He did efficient, clean work," said the man. The neighbor seemed pleased to have the recommendation and the number of a qualified plumber, but was a little startled when the man added, "He has a great personality, too!" Puzzled, the neighbor inquired, with a grin, "Was he fixing your sink or was he planning on moving in?" The point here is that plumbers should concentrate on things they are to repair and not on people and relationships. (They do get paid by the hour, you know!) In contrast, teachers should (we contend, *must*) focus on time-consuming relationships. We work with people, not things. If something is not functioning properly with our students, we can't simply replace them with a new and improved model; we have to work with what we have, the product as it comes to us. Part of what makes teaching difficult is that not everyone wants to be there. Unlike the world of work, where employees who don't like their jobs can quit, most students don't have that option. And neither do the teachers! Indeed, teaching must be about relationships! The heart of the professional ideal in teaching may well be a commitment to the ethic of caring. Caring requires more than bringing state-of-the-art technical knowledge to bear in one's practice. It means doing everything possible to enhance the learning, developmental, and social needs of students as persons. The heart of caring in schools is relationships with others (teacher, parent, and students) characterized by nurturance, altruistic love, and kinshiplike connections (Sergiovanni, 1994, p. 41).

Teaching and learning cannot occur without the teacher entering into a relationship with his or her students. In fact, the teacher's success in facilitating the learning process is directly related to the quality of that relationship. Let's look at it this way. Picture the significance of teacher rapport with students as one would think of flour in its relation to making a cake. If you've ever made a cake from scratch, you know the significance of one essential ingredient, the flour. Flour, that's simple, right? Did you know that not all flour is alike? There's self-rising flour, plain flour, wheat flour, bread flour, and many other types. If you attempt to make your cake with the wrong type of flour, then your end product will not be as you wish. Likewise, if we attempt to teach children without having the right kind of relationship with them, the end result will be very similar to baking a cake with bread flour.

We often fail to appreciate the importance of relationships; we have misconceptions about their significance to the teaching and learning process. Anderson (1985) points out that for thousands of years people theorized about the relationship between mind and learning. From this, many conclusions have been drawn about the nature of teaching. The earliest concepts we have of the mind are of "psyche," a Greek word for breath, because of the observed relationship between breathing and life. Without breathing, there is no life. Without relationships, there is no teaching.

Realistically, we know that learning is a process. The learning process yields optimum results when active participation on the part of the learner occurs. The teacher whose classroom embodies the keys to authentic learning—doing and not telling, immersion, familiarity and connections with the content, time for in-depth learning of concepts, engagement in an interactive community—creates this magic. You cannot force learning to happen any more than you can speed the growth of a plant by pulling on it. The learner must be given the opportunity to construct his or her own learning. The best we can do to help our students learn is to connect what we articulate to their previous experiences and knowledge. We should create an appropriate, stimulating environment in which our students can gradually construct their own understandings.

Teaching is inherently interactive because it depends on our abilities to make connections with our students. We make those connections through the perceived relationships we have with them. Effective teachers form relationships that are trustful, open, and secure. They share control with their students through methodology, such as cooperative groups, inquiry, and constructivist learning. These methods encourage interactions between the students in the classroom. The better the relationship, the better the interaction, hence the better the learning. Simply put, effective education takes place between a student and a teacher. For example:

> You must love the unlovable. Such wise words were once spoken to me and now are engraved on my heart for eternity. It was a life lesson, not just advice for a first-year teacher. In all my dealings with people, I will always remember that those who are hardest to love are the ones who need your love the most. This is certainly the case with one of my students. K. is an impish sort, dark haired and with a mischievous gleam in his eye. It has been a battle of the wits from day one. He tries my patience, tests my ability to overlook small annoyances, and has taught me to choose my battles very carefully.
>
> I keep in close contact with his mother; in fact, we communicate on a weekly basis. As I talk more and more with her, I learn more about K. He has a hard home life. K. is the oldest in his family and is expected to care for his younger siblings. He is also required to do much of the housework since his mother is pregnant with sibling number four. There is suspected abuse and anger management issues within the family. Here is a young boy that is expected to take on the responsibilities of a grown man! After speaking one afternoon to K.'s counselor, I returned to my classroom, shut the door, and sobbed until I had used up all of my tears. While blowing my nose, I vowed to love this child, no matter how many times he interrupted my lesson or came in late to homeroom in the morning. Every time he pulls away, I will push closer. We have finally come to the realization, after sheer exhaustion, that we are here for each other. He came into my life for love, and I came into his life for the same reason.
>
> (Beth Dodd, first-year teacher, seventh grade)

Once this first-year teacher was able to establish a connection with K., a relationship was formed and learning followed.

Another consideration in establishing positive relationships with students is to begin with our own inner self and to examine who we are as teachers. In his book *The Courage to Teach*, Palmer (1998) wrote that the premise of good teaching could not be reduced to one technique; rather, good teaching comes from the identity and integrity of the teacher. As an example of this premise, he describes his own teaching. In his classes he portrays his ability to connect with his students and to connect them with the subject matter as less dependent on his mastery of the subject matter and more dependent on the degree to which he trusts and shares his own self with his students. Good teachers are able to "weave a complex web of connections among themselves, their subjects, and their students so that students can learn to weave a world for themselves" (p. 11).

Modeling is also a mechanism for teachers to demonstrate integrity, the treatment of others, and the importance of relationships among others. Children learn by watching and observing others. William Morse (1994) wrote, "Deeper than management, teachers hope to change attitudes and even values in the confused and value-deficient youngsters. This requires the teacher to be a model, or deeper yet a figure for identification, one who interacts and discusses with children, pointing the way to more successful ways of feeling and acting" (p. 135). Much of how children behave and react to others around them is through emulating the behaviors of adults who play significant roles in their lives. We will not attempt to examine the results of modeling when children emulate what they view on television or in movies and what their peers say or do in the streets; rather, we will focus on the impact teachers play as role models. Students are more likely to model the behavior of people who are a major source of control, support, and nurturing. Students easily see through façades of teachers who expound the old saying of "do as I say and not as I do." If we are to be successful in our efforts of teaching students, we must be willing to deal with the affective as well as the cognitive components of the classroom. We must serve as positive role models in a way that facilitates students' personal growth while modeling emotional control and sensitivity to the needs of all students.

Teacher-student relationships tend to evolve into one of three types:

- Almost complete openness, in which we share a wide range of personal concerns and values with students.

- Openness to our reactions and feelings about the school environment, with limited sharing of aspects reflecting our out-of-school life.

- An almost exclusive focus on a role-bound relationship; that is, we share no personal feelings or reactions, but merely perform our instructional duties. (Jones, 1980)

Effective teachers are able to connect with their students on many levels. Students respond best to adults who are comfortable and confident with themselves, their values, and their interests. In truth, students respond best to teachers who are real. Geneal relays a story from her teaching career; it is about one time when she openly shared herself with her students.

Have you ever been in the grocery store or at Wal-Mart when one of your students sees you and calls out your name? Actually, yells would be a better description since everyone within sight turns to look at whom the student is yelling at! Or maybe you were out (out of school, that is) doing something for you (like jogging at the track to reduce your stress level) and then that student you most don't want to see outside of the classroom runs up to you and wants to jog along? Did you happen to catch the strange expression on his or her face? Something that says, "Gee, Mrs. Cantrell, I didn't know you went to the grocery store," "You eat Kraft macaroni and cheese?" or "You can jog?" If you teach long enough, this experience will certainly become a common one. It's to be expected. It is one of the hazards of the profession, I guess. But years ago, I had an unusual combination of students who actually became one of my greatest sources of strength during a very difficult period of my life.

It was late April and I had just received a call from my mother. She had gone to the doctor earlier in the day for what we thought were minor kidney problems. It turns out that her kidneys were failing and she was going to the hospital the following day for surgery to implant the apparatus for peritoneal dialysis. Prior to the surgery the doctors made the decision to place her on a dialysis machine to flush and clean her system for greater success in the surgery. However, during dialysis, her lungs began to fail (she was a heavy smoker) and her heart was beating far too fast (a couple of heart attacks to her credit) and she was rushed to the Intensive Care Unit (ICU) of the hospital with far more wrong that just kidney problems. She spent over 30 days in ICU on what could best be described for all parties involved as an emotional roller-coaster. It seemed that with each passing day, new and greater complications occurred and her chances of beating this illness grew slimmer.

Doctors make rounds in the ICU between seven and eight in the morning, which is not an easy time for a teacher to be away from school. However, I was fortunate to be teaching in a pull-out program for gifted and talented children, the hospital was only ten minutes from my school, and my classes didn't began until eight-thirty. I was even more fortunate to have a principal who allowed me to come in late each morning so I could go by the hospital to see my mother and hear the latest prognosis from her doctors. As soon as I arrived at school each day I would go and gather my cherubs to begin class.

As you might guess, many mornings when I arrived at school, I was still very distraught and upset over the latest news from the doctors. During this difficult period my students became my therapy. They would genuinely want to know how my mother was doing. I would talk and they would listen and almost without fail, I felt better after sharing my concerns and feelings with my students. I really don't know what I would have done without them.

Mom died in mid-July of that year. She never came home. Her last request was that she didn't want to die in the hospital. We were unable to grant her that last request. Although we knew she was never going to fully recover, her death was sudden and very difficult. During visitation at the funeral home, we had many friends and colleagues come and show their respect and to offer their help, support, and prayers. Between Greg's faculty and mine, there must have been hundreds of visitors. As the last friends were leaving and Greg and I were on our way out the door, I heard someone yell my name. And this time, I was elated to hear the sound of student voices. When I turned around I saw Stephen and Josh running toward me. They were two of my students who had listened and comforted me during my mom's stay in the hospital. They had just heard the news and rushed from baseball practice to see me. They wanted to come to make sure I was alright and to give me a big hug. They wanted to tell me how sorry they were that my mom had passed away and to assure me that everything would be fine.

Funny, I thought it was the teacher who was supposed to help her students. I found out differently that year; the relationship can work both ways.

In the ancient sense of the word, heart is the place where intellect, emotion, spirit, and will converge in the human self (Palmer, 1998). An important step in establishing positive relationships with our students is to remember who we are and why we chose to enter the profession; we need to remember the heart. Effective teachers don't have to share everything about their personal lives to be effective, but they need to share their passion and excitement for life and living and for the students in their care.

Getting to Know Your Students

After we "know thine own self" and understand who we are as teachers, we need to begin the daunting task of finding out about the students in our classrooms. Where do they live? Who do they live with? What are their learning styles? What are their personalities and interests? These are not always easy questions to answer and certainly ones that require time and effort on the part of the educator. Probably one of the biggest mistakes of past centuries in teaching has been to treat all children as if they were variants of the same individual, and thus to feel justified in teaching them the same subjects in the same way (Gardner, 1995). Without a doubt it is easier to treat all students as if they were the same by using the same worksheets, activities or methodology; but that is not what is best for all students. Basically, teachers of today are still faced with the same challenges with which teachers in one-room schoolhouses struggled. How do we divide our time, our resources, and our selves so we can be effective facilitators to maximize the learning potential of each student in our charge? Is it even possible? The following reflection serves as an example of a frustrated first-year teacher's inability to understand and relate to her students.

I was glad that our induction class met yesterday and really learned a lot from some of the articles the girls [other first-year teachers] did. I have also been thinking about what we talked about concerning that one child in my class whose home life has affected his motivation. I mean, I didn't mean to sound so hateful or uncaring about my student when I said what if I don't want to tell him that I won't give up on him. What if I already have given up and his very presence in my class upsets me. Honestly, when I think about John and everything I've been through with him, it's hard to keep a positive outlook. His home situation is not ideal and that really bothers me because I can't change that!!! I have no control over the fact that he does not have a positive male role model at home. Yes, John's grandfather is there but he always sounds drunk and he's mean. I know because I've talked to him a few times. His grandmother works a lot and I feel that by the time she gets home in the evening she doesn't have much to give this little boy or she just doesn't care, either. I don't know. All I know is that he sits through my class day in and day out and doesn't do much at all. I'm tired of dealing with that and with the fact that I don't know what else to do. It bothers me that I get so frustrated with him and my attitude turns negative. Like you said, this job is so emotional and I feel responsible for him, yet what else can I do for him? How do I motivate him to realize that in his precious life it's going to be up to him to do what it takes to succeed? I mean, his parents have shown me that they don't care about his educational success for whatever reason so he's going to have to be the one to care, right?

Like many teachers, the induction teacher in the above reflection is frustrated with meeting the needs of students in her charge. How do you teach students like John? The induction teacher has some knowledge about John and certainly has tried to reach him but unfortunately to no avail. Sadly, John is just one in a classroom of 25. Glasser (1990) describes teaching as difficult, even under the best educational circumstances. He continues to say that it is our failure to take into account the needs of students that makes what is already a difficult job almost impossible. Any method of teaching that ignores the needs of teachers and students is bound to fail. To accomplish what we need to in our classrooms today, we must place student interests at the center of school reform, not textbooks, not standards, and certainly not standardized testing. Effective teachers unconditionally accept students as they are and attempt to address their individual needs. A first-year teacher reflects on how she strived to meet the needs of the students in her first grade classroom.

This year, one of the most important things I have done is to learn to treat each child as an individual. Before I even began the year, one of my goals was to get to know each child and learn their needs. Every child in every classroom is different, and therefore every child needs to be treated differently. It is very important to learn how each child learns best, but before a child can even begin learning you have to learn how to work with them and to get them to work with you. Some of my students came into first grade ready to learn, while others were so far from ready that I was not quite sure how in the world I was going to deal with them. All of my students have come so far academically and behaviorally, but one student stands out in my mind when looking at how far he has come from the beginning of the year. I did not know what I was going to do with him, no matter how much I loved this student; he frustrated me to the point of tears.

I have written about Q. before, and even after almost eight months he still fascinates me. He was so immature when he came into school and throughout the year, it seemed just as I got his attention and all was going smoothly, something else would come up and throw everything off. I treat Q. very differently than every other student in my classroom. Actually I treat all of my students differently, but I think it is very apparent to many people the difference in the way I treat Q. The wonderful group of children I teach have adjusted and they also treat him differently. He needs a lot more attention than any other student in the classroom, actually more than any student I have ever encountered. He is such a sweet and bright child, but has had a very difficult time focusing on what actually needs to be done each day. Q. often has a problem with just saying whatever might be on his mind at the moment, whenever he feels it necessary to tell me. At first this was very disturbing, but for the most part I have learned to respond to him and remind him that he can tell me all about it at lunch when he sits next to me.

Q. also has had a very difficult time finishing his work, but his mom, Q., and I have made a special agreement that consists of rewards for every time he gets his work done for the day. It has worked perfectly so far and I am slowly lessening the rewards so that his motivation will no longer be so external, but rather internal. I have realized that he needs special little things and special moments of attention in order for him and the others to learn in my classroom. When Q. has been disruptive in the past, it disrupts the whole class from learning. He easily draws attention to himself, which has succeeded in throwing off everyone who is trying to accomplish anything at the moment. Yet even though it has taken all of my patience at times to figure out how to deal with him, it has been worth it because I have learned so much about him, and he has affected my life in so many ways.

I know that this class will always hold a special place in my heart because it was my first class, but I also know that Q. has his own place in my heart and always will. He has helped me realize the importance of getting to know each child in one's classroom. There were times I thought he would never learn and that I was going to have a nervous breakdown, but now he has proven me wrong. He is one of the 19 reasons I like to get up in the morning to go to school and teach. When he is missing or any of my other students are missing, my day is not the same. He may never know the effect he has had on me and he may not remember this year very clearly, but I will always remember him whenever I have a challenging student. When I think of him I will remember never to give up on any of my students because there is always a way to get through to them. You just have to look inside them long and hard to find it!

(Mindy Sokolowski, first-year teacher)

Certainly, one of the major roadblocks to meeting the individual needs of our students is time. It takes time to make a home visit, time to place a phone call, time to engage in dialogue with colleagues concerning students, time to administer and evaluate student interest inventories, time to determine student learning styles, and time to keep anecdotal records. But the time invested is essential in our quest to meet the needs of the students in our classrooms. Ponder this—a student comes to you with a hurt leg (let's say a learning disability) and you rush right in to help him. Experience has provided you with a long list of strategies and approaches to help strengthen and heal the wounded leg (modify assignments, teach using a variety of methods, or individualize).

However, in your haste to fix the hurt leg, not once did you stop to find out any other information about the student. In doing so you totally missed the "severed hand" (parents are divorced, mother is an alcoholic, enrolled in the fourth school this year, slight hearing problem). Over time, because of your failure to really get to know and understand the student, he "bled to death." This is a grim analogy, but one that is all too true in far too many classrooms. Students who are placed in classrooms where teachers do not take the time to identify their needs often fall through the cracks and are lost to the system.

Importance of Community in the Classroom

In conjunction with identifying the unique and distinctive needs of students in the classroom, teachers must also create a community among the learners in the class. In creating community in the classroom, you are growing a learning space. The blending of caring and order enables educators to meet students' personal needs. Both are essential for teachers to create a safe and positive learning environment. In his book *Improving Schools from Within*, Ronald Barth (1990) wrote:

> What needs to be improved about schools is their culture, the quality of interpersonal relationships, and the nature and quality of learning experiences. School improvement is an effort to determine and provide, from without and within, conditions under which adults and youngsters who inhabit schools will promote and sustain learning among themselves. By building community in schools we increase the likelihood that capacity will be tapped, conditions will become right, and the culture of the school will be improved. (p. 45)

It is the teacher's assignment to create an organizational climate that will increase the chances for learner success. Trust and openness serve as the foundation upon which learners and teachers build such communities. When teachers listen to, observe, and ask questions of students, they model the interest and caring they want their students to demonstrate as well. Dewey (1916/1994) was one of the earliest educators to envision the role of schooling as preparing students for problem solving and democratic, rational living. If students are to become socially responsible adults, they have to participate in planning, creating, and evaluating their learning experiences in school. Life in the classroom, according to Dewey, should be a democracy in microcosm. The school cannot become a total learning organization until it becomes a community of learners. Community is necessary because students need a supportive learning environment, one that is virtually risk free in order to pursue standards of high intellectual quality (Keefe & Jenkins, 1997). If we are to create meaningful changes in our schools, we need to pay attention to the quality of the relationships and the quality of life in our schools. No educational change will have a meaningful impact if we do not simultaneously work to create more democratic, personally engaging, caring and supportive learning environments for teachers and students (Jones & Jones, 1998). In creating communities in our classrooms we increase the quality of the learning environment and ultimately the success and futures of our students.

High Expectations

School effectiveness research has consistently pointed to teachers' high expectations of student performance as a key factor connected to a student's achievement. Simply stated, you get what you expect. Teachers who anticipate that their students will not perform well find that indeed they will not. If teachers expect, require, and encourage students to perform in a quality manner, they usually do.

So how does this expectation to perform actually work as it relates to teacher and student interactions? Teachers who say, "I have high expectations for my students," and yet structure the classroom in such a way that the students don't believe or respond to these expectations is no more effective than the teacher who, from the beginning, conveys the attitude that his or her students cannot achieve or behave in any way other than that which their background, culture or other labels dictate. Neither teacher will allow the student to move beyond a preconceived point of success.

We believe that high expectations are essential in a well-ordered and organized classroom. Those teachers who are successful in relating to their students convey through those relationships a confident belief that you can do it. The environment of trust, understanding, and knowledge of the students' own dreams and aspirations permeates this type of classroom. Has the clash of standards-driven curriculum and high-stakes testing with the growing diversity in America's classrooms produced an environment where students are labeled and expectations established commensurate with their labels? Has the current state of many of our classrooms produced teachers who no longer help students to strive toward their dreams but just move them along in an assembly-line fashion? The following story helps to illustrate this concept:

> Once upon a time, there was a large mountainside where an eagle's nest rested. The nest contained four large eagle eggs. One day an earthquake rocked the mountain, causing one of the eggs to roll down the mountain into the chicken farm below. The chickens decided that they must nurture and care for the eagle's egg, so an old hen volunteered to raise the large eagle egg.

One day the egg hatched and a beautiful eagle was born. Although it was evident that the eagle was not a chicken, he was raised to become a chicken. After a time the eagle believed that he was nothing more than just a chicken. The eagle loved his home and his family, but his spirit cried out for more. While playing a game on the farm one day, the eagle looked at the skies above and noticed a group of mighty eagles soaring overhead. "Oh," the eagle cried, "I wish I could soar like those birds." His siblings all laughed and said, "You cannot soar with those birds, you are a chicken. Chickens do not soar!"

The eagle continued staring at his real family above, dreaming that he could be with them. Each time the eagle would let his dreams be known, he was told he couldn't be like those birds. Eventually he gave up and that is what the eagle learned to believe. The eagle stopped dreaming. After a long life as a chicken, the eagle passed away.

The moral of this story: You become what you believe you are. Don't be like the eagle; follow your dreams!

How many times do teachers stifle the dreams and aspirations of their students? How many times do we tell students with both words and actions that they can't complete a task, do well on an assignment, or go on to college? Do our expectations, or lack thereof, prevent students from maximizing their potential? In a classroom with an honest, open, caring environment the likelihood of "eagles believing that they are chickens," a belief presented either by the teacher or by the students' classmates, is remote. It is in this arena that an effective teacher's students excel by encouragement and realistic individual high expectations.

However, there is a concern when high expectations without relationship development and a true knowledge of the student exist. This situation can create a classroom that is just as frustrating to the teacher and students as one who labels students openly as "chickens and eagles." While the authors caution that knowledge of students should never be used as an excuse for high expectations, the understanding of the student's home and family environment is critical to the establishment of realistically established expectations. This is especially true for many out-of-school activities such as homework. The following story serves as a personal illustration of this concept.

As any principal of any school for a prolonged length of time will tell you, it is not unusual to have previously learned and definitely experienced knowledge of particular families of children in your school. This was certainly true of the H. family who had both "blessed and cursed" my school for years as students, parents, the parent's children and even their grandchildren matriculated through the grades. As principal of a large school, it is also a fairly common occurrence for teachers in a moment of frustration when their high expectations of students fail to work out that they complain to the principal about a particular student who falls into this noncompliance category. "He won't do anything in my class and I want you to do something about it!"

First, let me say that issues of noncompliance with regard to academic endeavors such as homework, bringing materials to class, and so on are personally viewed as motivation problems rather than as discipline problems. Some teachers, however, take these issues very seriously. They view them as personal attacks to their authority in the classroom: "He is not completing my work!"

One of these occurrences sets the stage for the story of T. H. As stated earlier, the H. family was well known in the school community. You name it and they've done it! Late fall, a particular teacher had great concerns about T. H. and his inability or desire to complete his homework. This was manifested in negative conversations between the teacher and student, as well as with a marked increase in T. H.'s office referrals. As principal, I became aware of the situation and tried to intervene first by speaking with T. H. about his "school responsibilities" and second by "educating" the teacher.

Following an emotional interaction with the teacher regarding T. H.'s continued noncompliance with her homework policy, I decided that it was time for a "field trip." I invited the teacher to meet me during her planning period in the school parking lot. We got into my 1980 Ford Courier truck and proceeded to leave for the H. house. Having been there many times in negative situations, I worried about the reaction of the family upon my arrival, but quickly dismissed this concern over the benefit of the visit for my staff member in her own professional development.

As we traveled down the long dirt drive toward the H. home, which requires four-wheel drive capability, I stopped to tell my teacher that I appreciated her efforts and expectations for T. H., but I felt that she needed a more complete picture of his background. As we approached the house I sensed her concern and escalating apprehension. After we arrived at the small, unpainted wooden framed house, I could tell that she was nervous.

We exited my truck and went up the steps to the porch, which included a large hole just in front of the door. Given that it was still warm, the front door was wide open with no screen door in sight (and no screens on the windows, either). The open door gave easy access to all of the family animals that were taking full advantage of going in and out of the house at will. Mrs. H. greeted us and we entered the stark surroundings of the four-room house that consisted of a living area, a kitchen, bedroom, and bathroom. Littering the floor and stacked in corners around the room were bedrolls. Mrs. H. shared with us the fact that 11 people resided in the house. After giving us more insight on the struggles she was having running the household, the teacher and I left. When we climbed into my truck to return to school, I said, rather matter-of-factly, "Now, Mrs. "X," just where exactly is T. H. supposed to do your homework each night?" Immediately, the teacher looked at me and began to sob. All she could say was, "I had no idea he lived like that." Not much other conversation occurred during the trip back to school; actually, not much needed to be said.

Following the field trip, the teacher certainly did not lessen her expectations for T. H., but she *did* alter the procedural expectations for him. Sometimes she met him early at school and had breakfast with him to help him complete his homework or she stayed late and took him home. His office visits from this point forward were few and far between. Her personal relationship with him improved, immensely impacting his attitude and his grades.

Often we get caught up in standards, policies, rules, school culture, and self, and fail to see the impact that all of our daily contacts with students have, not only on their futures but also on ours. Like the teacher described, we can in fact have high expectations for each of our students if we truly *know* our students.

Conclusion

We strongly believe that positive relationship development is the single most important aspect of all human relations and that the classroom is certainly an environment within which this concept is paramount. Effective teachers understand, or at least demonstrate this fact every day in their classrooms.

The title of this chapter, "Kids don't care how much you know 'til they know how much you care," pretty much says it all. Students gravitate, learn from, and most certainly remember teachers who live by this credo. It is this event that establishes, in many respects, a student's success or failure in school. Understanding this opens the door to a more effective and mutually rewarding student and teaching learning experience.

CHAPTER 2

You Have to Get the Hog's Attention Before You Can Load Him on the Truck!

Student Motivation

One of the most frequently asked questions in education, especially by novice teachers, is "How do I get my students to do what they need to do?" The response to this burning question really is quite simple. "Motivate them!" Yet, in reality, discovering how to do that may seem more elusive than the never-ending search for the Holy Grail! As we began our quest for discovering how to motivate students, we found that numerous studies, strategies, and findings do not lead to any magic formula. We then turned to veteran teachers to identify strategies and theories of motivation they utilized; most could not name a theory or identify how to actually do it. Competent teachers just seem to motivate students instinctively without practicing any singular theoretical approach.

What are the keys to effective motivation? Is there a simple solution to motivation in the classroom? Or is the problem a very complex series of intertwined events? Why are some students easier to motivate than others? Are schools the basis for the increasing malady of unmotivated students? The pressure of high-stakes testing and accountability has pushed schools to look for measures to pound standards into the minds of our students. Consequently, are current educational practices actually the reason why some students don't appear to want to learn? These are not easy questions to answer, especially when you consider the last. People from the business sector, parents, politicians, and presidents have begun to sound like the proverbial broken record with the rhetoric that almost anything can be done to students and to schools, no matter how ill-considered, as long as it is done in the name of "raising standards" or "accountability." One is reminded of how politicians, faced with the perception of high crime rates, resort to the get-tough mentality of lock 'em up, by the book, law and order. This response plays well with the general public, but is based on an exaggeration of the problem, a misanalysis of its causes, and simplistic prescription that frequently ends up doing more harm than good. When this same mentality is applied to America's schools, harm is definitely the result of these procedures.

The debate over the efficacy of changing schools and schooling transcends normal boundaries. It is increasingly difficult to tell Democrats from Republicans, liberals from conservatives, and even parents from business entrepreneurs on the issue of accountability in our schools and school systems. Virtually each group clearly believes in the need to change schools and schooling. We do not disagree that schools, in fact, do need to change, but (and this is very important) left out almost entirely in this dialogue are the very dedicated educators and especially the students themselves. It is this consideration that has the greatest impact on students and their learning!

Regardless of any discussion, from coast to coast, and north to south, the teaching practices that help students understand ideas from their deepest conceptual origins and create an environment that fosters the sustaining of student interest and understandings are under siege. The following is an excellent summary of this very concept:

> Not long ago, a widely respected middle school teacher, renowned for helping students design their own innovative learning projects, stood up in a meeting to discuss the school's "accountability report card" and said, "I used to be a good teacher." The room fell silent at the use of the past tense. "These days," he explained, "I just hand out textbooks and quiz my students on what they have memorized. The reason is simple: My colleagues and I are increasingly held accountable for raising test scores." He continued, "The kind of wide-ranging and enthusiastic exploration of ideas that once characterized my classroom could no longer take place when the sole emphasis of teaching and learning revolved around preparation for the standardized test."

How sad! We have begun to dismantle the art of teaching down to prescribing memorization of facts. The purveyors of standards and accountability without equally emphasizing creative teaching are winning, and for that reason the students are losing!

Kincheloe (1995) refers to this phenomenon as "factoid syndrome." Factoid syndrome occurs when students are required to memorize isolated facts and figures only to spit them out for the mandated test. Students are not allowed to digest the information or question its relevance, process, or connection to previous learning; alas, there are too many standards to be "covered." Other than playing a mean game of jeopardy or making it past the first tier of questions on *Who Wants To Be a Millionaire*, our colleague Denise Crockett would ask, "So what?" Whatever answers to this question and others might be, motivation appears to be one of the top concerns of most teachers. Listen to the voice of this first-year teacher:

> I've been teaching for nearly one month now. In some ways it has gone by so fast and in other ways it seems to have dragged on! I am so tired by the time I get home at the

end of the school day. For the most part, I am adjusting well to the new surroundings but I am still awed by the responsibility that I have to the students, their parents, and the school. Will my students learn what it is they need to learn before the end of the school year? Am I doing the right things? Are they actually learning anything? Am I making a difference?

The biggest issue with which I have struggled the most so far is unmotivated students. How in the world do you motivate students that for the most part have no desire to be in school, much less in your classroom? This has been my greatest challenge yet. One particular student comes to mind. I'll call him Eric. He is a good kid for the most part and, actually, he's not too much of a discipline problem. He just doesn't participate in class or do his classwork unless I am in close proximity and keeping an eye on him. Not a simple task with 27 students! I know he is smart and is capable of doing the assignments. I've moved him to the front of the room and that has helped some. I've talked to his mother many times but even she has given up on him. When I talk to him about his future and how important school is he acts like he doesn't care! I'm at my wits' end if you know what I mean! What can I do if they don't even care?

That's a good question and not an easy one to answer! Seasoned teachers usually answer that question with a puzzled look on their face and respond, "I don't know how I get them to do their work, they just do!" Our question then is this: What exactly is it that they do to motivate their students? As we attempt to answer this question, let's first look at a definition of motivation.

Definition of Motivation

Motivation is more than just completing a worksheet, turning in a book summary, doing what the teacher says, or making good grades; it is a craving to discover, understand, and appreciate knowledge and schooling. Simply stated, motivation is the student's desire to learn. Among other things, desire to learn can be affected by whether the student believes he or she will be successful at the task, whether he or she has interest in the subject matter, or the degree to which he or she values the rewards associated with the task itself (Feather, 1982). It is also important to note that even though students may appear to be equally involved in the task at hand, their ultimate motivation toward the final product will most likely differ. Before proceeding, further let's consider a reflection from an intern who is completing an early experience at a school during her senior year.

Being in private school for 12 years certainly prepared me for college but I was in no way prepared for what was the reality of our nation's public school system when I observed it in my middle school today. What I witnessed in the classroom was abhorrent. The standards and expectations of today's students have hit an all-time low. Children are being bribed to do the bare minimum and rewarded simply for doing what they have been instructed to do. Responsibility and accountability mean nothing, and according to one source from the school, students cannot fail a grade or be held back. With a policy like that, we are basically telling the kids that they can do as little work as they want and still get by. Isn't this ultimately hurting the children? And the fact that my co-teacher has to bribe her students with points and candy simply to write down their homework assignments is appalling. When I was in school, writing down assignments wasn't even a question in our minds, doing the assignments was never optional, nor was it acceptable to turn work in late. In fact, us "overachievers" feared the consequences of our work not being perfectly correct and flawless.

Maybe I am an idealistic perfectionist whose standards are unrealistic and whose expectations seem unattainable, but this vicious cycle of no responsibility or accountability needs to be broken. While accommodation is important, the bar needs to stay raised and the expectations need to remain high.

Do you agree? Is this an all-too-common occurrence in our classrooms? What motivational techniques are being employed in this classroom? The frustrations of this preservice teacher are not just her concerns but also those of many educators in the field. Are we doing our students more harm by attempting to trick them into school? Indeed in this classroom it appears that extrinsic motivation may be doing more harm than good. The response to this preservice teacher from her university supervisor follows.

Thanks for sharing and for being so open and honest with your reaction to your first week at school. Please try to keep your eyes open as you continue going to your school placement. I really do think it is a great place and once you've been there awhile I think you will agree. Teaching is not easy. I've said that many times; but it is worth it! Hang in there; I predict you, too, will learn to love middle school kids just like me. You are so right about learning their names quickly. I'm happy to hear that you are working hard on that. Students will not care until they know you care and learning their names is an important step in doing that. Speaking to students at the end of class by standing in the doorway to say good-bye sounds so simple to you and me but it really can make a difference in your relationships with your students. It would be great if later when football season begins you could go see a game, stay for a pep rally, or something similar. Doing those things means much more to them than you or I will ever know. Yes [student] you are being idealistic on your expectations of middle school students but I actually think that is a good thing. I would much rather see you have high expectations and standards instead of giving up and accepting the unacceptable. I caution you to keep in mind that this is early in the year and some of the things that you perceive [the co-teacher] to be doing as "bribing" may be what she has to do to win them over. At this age, huge walls are forming around them [middle school students]…they've been hurt or disappointed by too many adults and this is just one way they cope and test you. What appears to be giving up or not caring is their way of being in control and having power. This is real hard for me to explain in e-mail but I would love to talk to you about it one day.

I hope that with time you will see your students as more than just "a group" and see them as individuals who have individual needs. You haven't had me in class yet, but for those who have, they can tell you I feel strongly that we teach students and not subjects.

Remember, if you can't reach them, you can't teach them. Search for ways to do just that!

As stated at the beginning of this chapter, the search for answers to what motivates students is not easy. The frustration of this teacher candidate's desire to seek the source of apparent student apathy and question the use of external motivators is real. Those of us who have been in the profession for a number of years can identify with her frustrations. Experience in today's classrooms yields one clear message—there are no quick fixes to motivating children to succeed in school. Often we feel compelled to play the game, as the co-teacher mentioned in the reflection. We want to give our preservice and induction teachers "the solution" because they believe there is one! But in order to develop a clear understanding, one has to think about the bigger picture, the true purpose of schools. Kincheloe (1995) speaks of schools in a democratic society; schools that exist to help students locate themselves in history, obtain the ability to direct their own lives, understand the ways power influences the production of knowledge, and connect with a cognitive revolution that leads to a deeper understanding of themselves in the world (p. 127).

So, do schools, in fact, see themselves in this light? Have schools turned to an elitist view of education, which is based on those students who can perform in the current system and those who cannot? Have we mandated a culture in our schools and classrooms that ignores the differences that exist naturally in the same classrooms? These are valid questions. If we know what we know, then why do we not do what we should do? Student motivation hinges greatly on some basic principles that we will discuss later in this chapter. However, to disregard what we know about teaching and learning is a sure path to completing the demise of American education.

As the nation's school populations shift to a more racially, culturally, linguistically, ethnically, and socioeconomically diverse composition of students with diverse life experiences, the population of teachers grows more homogeneous. It is this single fact that should drive us to respond in a concerted effort to begin to change our approach to accepting and operationalizing the ominous task of teaching America's young.

Types of Motivation

> Typically, the information offered to teachers about motivational strategies focuses on controlling performance rather than on stimulating motivation to learn, and emphasizes the use of incentives, rewards, and grades rather than strategies designed to stimulate students to generate learning goals and the cognitive and metacognitive strategies to accomplish them.
>
> —Jere Brophy (1986)

In response to demands to improve classroom climate, increase student learning, and invite school success, many strategies found their way into our schools in the form of behavior modification. Later, behaviorists developed and promoted techniques derived from reinforcement theory. Humanistic educators encouraged teachers to focus on developing self-concept, meeting individual needs, and encouraging student progress. Basically these theories fall into two simple categories of student motivation—intrinsic and extrinsic. Students who are intrinsically motivated tackle a task or assignment for its own sake. This may be for the enjoyment it may provide from participating in the activity, or for the feeling of a sense of accomplishment. Conversely, extrinsically motivated students usually perform an activity for an external reward (stickers, candy, grades, etc.) or to avoid some type of punishment (loss of recess, office referral, etc.).

Although any kind of motivation seems preferable to none, there is compelling evidence that students who are more intrinsically than extrinsically motivated fare better (Brooks et al., 1998). In fact, some research demonstrates that using extrinsic motivators to engage students in learning can both lower achievement and negatively affect student motivation (Dev, 1997; Lumsden, 1994). Students who are motivated to complete a task only to avoid consequences or to earn a certain grade rarely exert more than the minimum effort necessary to meet their goal. And when students are focused on comparing themselves with their classmates, rather than mastering skills at their own rate, they are more easily discouraged and their intrinsic motivation to learn may actually decrease. Brooks et al. (1998) observe that while external rewards may sustain productivity, they "decrease interest in the task, thereby diminishing the likelihood that the task will be continued in the future" (p. 26).

On the other hand, students who are intrinsically motivated finish ahead in a number of areas. Intrinsically motivated students have a propensity to:

- Earn higher grades and achievement test scores on average than extrinsically motivated students (Dev, 1997; Skinner & Belmont, 1991).

- Be better personally adjusted to school (Skinner & Belmont, 1991).

- Employ strategies that demand more effort and that enable them to process information more deeply (Lumsden, 1994).

- Be more likely to feel confident about their ability to learn new material (Dev, 1997).

- Use more logical information-gathering and decision-making strategies than do extrinsically motivated students (Lumsden, 1994).

- Be more likely to engage in tasks that are moderately challenging, whereas extrinsically oriented students gravitate toward tasks that are low in degree of difficulty (Lumsden, 1994).

- Be more likely to persist with and complete assigned tasks (Dev, 1997).

- Retain information and concepts longer, and are less likely to need remedial courses and review (Dev, 1997).

- Be more likely to be lifelong learners, continuing to educate themselves outside the formal school setting long after external motivators such as grades and diplomas are removed (Kohn, 1993).

Which method of motivation is the correct, intrinsic or extrinsic? Ironically, there is some objection as to whether students can be described as either intrinsically or extrinsically motivated. Sternberg and Lubart (1995), for example, argue that this division is too simple to mirror the many complex and interrelated factors that influence a student's motivation to succeed in school. They point out that most successful people are actually motivated by both internal and external factors, and suggest that educators should build on both types when working to engage students more fully in school.

Probably the most recognized name among researchers in the field of motivation is Jere Brophy. His definition of motivation to learn is that it is a competence acquired through personal experience but stimulated most directly through modeling, communication of expectations, and direct instruction or socialization by significant others (especially parents and teachers). As Brophy points outs, the child's home environment shapes the initial formation of attitudes the child develops regarding learning. When parents encourage and nurture their child's natural inquisitiveness and curiosity about the world by welcoming their questions, encouraging exploration and familiarizing them with the resources that they can use to enlarge their world, they are giving them the message that learning is worthwhile and frequently fun and satisfying. This is the basis for the internalization of intrinsically motivated characteristics in students.

Once school starts, children begin to solidify their beliefs about school-related successes and failures. Walter Doyle (1983) wrote that the quality of the time students spend engaged in academic work depends on the tasks they are expected to accomplish and the extent to which students understand what they are doing. It is essential, therefore, that direct instruction include explicit attention to meaning and not simply focus on engagement as an end in itself (p. 189). Certainly, this confirms the degree to which students perceive and feel their successes and failures have important implications for how they approach and cope with future learning situations.

School in its formal setting is the most powerful factor in solidifying how a child feels about his or her academic worth. However, teachers committed to children's learning and social development must be concerned about the power of cultural, social, economic, and political dynamics in shaping children's education futures and about creating a teaching force dedicated to fairness, equity, and social justice. What is currently at stake is not just the narrow view of academic achievement as the total school mission, but a school preparation that embraces goals of work, culture, and freedom. Fulfilling the promise of children's powerful learning to promote their participation in a multiracial, multiethnic democracy challenges us to reconsider what is important for teachers to know and be able to do.

Culturally responsive teaching would advocate creating a learning environment where students feel respected, valued, and challenged for their individuality. Students need to feel safe and nurtured, encouraged to take risks, participate in class discussions, and participate in the learning process. We purport that it is essential to create an interactive, constructivistic, personalized approach to learning. Such an approach to motivation in the classroom is embracing the notion that motivation is indeed an individual act.

An Individual Act

If you subscribe to the term "motivation" as the focusing of energy that is caused by a desire or a need, and further believe that all people, including students, are intrinsically motivated to learn, then we have a basis for what we believe great teachers do to motivate their students. Indeed, all students are motivated to learn; they just don't always want to learn what we want them to! That does not diminish what we are trying to teach, but it does focus our challenge on how we create a classroom that unlocks our students' intrinsic motivation to learn and channels their energy toward lifelong learning and to making the connection between teaching and learning.

Perhaps we should rephrase our initial question from "How do I get my students to do what they need to do?" to "What is it that motivates my students and how can I use that in my teaching so my students will want to learn and be successful?" This shift in thought implies that motivation is indeed an individual event. That is, the one-size-fits-all mentality just does not work. Imagine teaching all our students in exactly the same way, at the same time, at the same speed, using the same strategies. That's a sad thought but unfortunately one that is far too often actualized! One possible alternative might be to motivate each one individually, rather than "just motivate them."

The shift toward contextual teaching is necessary to achieve the idea of individualized student motivation. This concept, simply put, is the approach to teaching and learning that helps teachers relate subject matter to real-world situations and motivates students to make connections between knowledge and its application to their lives as family members, citizens, and workers and to engage in the hard work that learning requires. Contextual teaching and learning emphasizes problem solving, recognizes that teaching and learning can occur in a variety of places, encourages and teaches students to monitor and direct their own learning, anchors teaching in student's diverse life contexts, encourages students to learn from one another, and employs authentic assessment. Extending to all children this path of learning relates not just to what we think about teaching and learning, but also to the social context, the institutional nature of schools, and teachers' images of what learners can do.

This ability to vary the individual nature of motivation is the first mark of a great teacher. Although some tried, true, and canned motivation techniques do work in some classrooms, motivation is still for the most part an individual event. Let's look at the classic story of *The Wizard of Oz*. The main characters (Scarecrow, Tin Man, Cowardly Lion, and Dorothy Gail) were all searching for what they perceived to be the key to their happiness. As the story goes, the answer to this dream could only be found at the Emerald City. After surviving the many dangers and hardships along the Yellow Brick Road, the four finally arrived at the Land of Oz. They were told they must deliver the broom of the Wicked Witch of the West before they could meet the wizard and ask for their wishes to be granted. During the climactic presentation of the broom to the wizard, Toto exposed the wizard for what he truly was, a fraud. All were angry and hurt, but most of all disappointed. It was then that the wizard convinced each one that what he or she wanted most could be found inside the individual. The Scarecrow wanted a brain. It was his wit and cleverness that led the group to defeat the Wicked Witch; for this he was awarded a diploma. The Tin Man was given a heart-shaped clock that ticked for his acts of kindness and love that he demonstrated numerous times throughout the story. And let's not forget the Cowardly Lion, whose wish was to have courage so he could truly be the king of the forest; he received a medal for his efforts in the end to save Dorothy Gail from the Wicked Witch. That leaves Dorothy Gail. As it turns out, Dorothy Gail had the ability all along to go home to Kansas. She simply needed to click her ruby slippers together three times and repeat the words "there's no place like home."

In some ways, teachers may need to be more like the wizard. We must be able to identify the individual gifts of our students, and more importantly, like the wizard, point those out to them. This implies that the necessary time should be spent to identify these hidden talents and to incorporate them into the instructional planning and thus improve student performance, classroom environment, and student as well as teacher satisfaction. Are we teaching our teachers this concept or do they have to painfully experience this through failure? Geneal relates a personal story from her first year of teaching that illustrates this concept.

As far back as I can remember I had fond memories of approaching each school year with renewed vigor and zeal. I was the type of student who as soon as summer was out was counting down the days for the next school year to begin. Each June I was busy gathering and organizing my new school supplies for the following school year. I think it would be safe to say that I have always been a highly motivated learner. I was every teacher's ideal dream student. I was self-directed. I always had my homework, I always followed the directions, and I always completed my projects and papers well ahead of time. (Greg and I have two children; one was born seven weeks early and the other three weeks early; need I say more?) I graduated from high school as valedictorian of my class and magna cum laude in college from a teacher preparation program. I was ready to conquer the world! And then I encountered my first classroom.

My first teaching position was to teach math to students in grades four through eight in a very rural, very poor region of South Carolina. This means that my first position had me placed as a migrant teacher; I not only moved from room to room, I also moved from school to school. I was at the elementary school in the morning and the middle school in the afternoon. But, that was fine with me; I was fresh out of college, eager to put into practice all the methods, strategies, and techniques I had learned from my education professors. It's probably important that you know that this position began in January, well after everything had been established, both good and bad. The day finally arrived when I met my students! Nothing that I had done or seen or lived had prepared me for what I stumbled upon in the first days of school.

I found a wide range of students of varying levels of abilities, varying backgrounds, and most certainly, varying levels of motivation. My college professors had prepared me for the challenges concerning the differences in background and abilities of students, but the issue that proved to be my biggest challenge was motivation. I was at a total loss regarding how to work with students who did not want to be at school.

As I've already stated, I was a highly motivated student. In fact, most of my friends were highly motivated; it was almost a friendly competition among the group to see who made the highest grades. My students would not complete their classwork much less bring in homework the following day. They competed to see who received the lowest grades! When I tried to talk to them about how important school was to their future, responses ranged from none to those that aren't appropriate to repeat in mixed company. Very early on in my first teaching experience I became frustrated. I began to question whether I had made the right choice about going into the teaching profession. It's only the second week of school and already I am a failure, I thought. Was there not anything in my past that I could pull from to help me motivate these kids? And then I recalled a story.

All my life I have lived in the South. Currently, I am living in the house I grew up in. Among the many things that I cherish about my southern heritage are the traditions. In my family, one of the most prevalent and prevailing traditions was that of Sunday lunch. Every Sunday you were expected to go to church and then gather around the table for a hearty, down-home meal. Generally, it was the only meal served on Sundays. This ritual continued even after my older brothers were married and I was in college. My boyfriend, soon to be my future husband, was also included in those events. One particular Sunday my father announced that after lunch he had some work to do at the processing plant. The task this day was to load some pigs onto the trailer for sale the following day. So, trying to find his niche in the family, my future husband volunteered to go and offer a helping hand to my dad. Being the proud daughter of a meat packer, the tendencies of animals, especially farm animals, were almost second nature to me. And I knew that what sounded like an easy task was not and that Greg was in for a rude awakening.

My two older brothers went along with my dad and Greg. They got in the truck and ventured down to the pig parlor. The privilege of prodding the pigs to get on the truck was given to Greg and he was very eager to successfully complete the task. Today, there were five pigs to load. Almost as soon as the trailer was backed up and the door opened, the first pig all but ran on the truck, anxious and ready to accept the assignment that was before him. The second was a little more hesitant but as soon as Greg approached him, he walked up the ramp to the truck. The third pig squealed and complained but with a good long stare ventured up the ramp. The fourth pig only made his way up the ramp when Greg walked over and picked up a hickory switch. All Greg had to do was show the switch to the pig and he ran up the ramp. There was only one pig left, and Greg said, "I don't know why you thought you needed so much help, this is easy." And then he looked over to the corner of the pen to get his first glimpse of pig number five. Actually, I think this pig is what one refers to down South as a hog, weighing in at well over 400 pounds.

Well, Greg thought, I've already discovered several methods of motivation that work, so why not try those that are tried and true? He tentatively walked toward the hog; no luck, he didn't budge. He moved on to the stare, tried raising his voice, told the hog to get on the truck, asked the hog politely, and finally waved the switch in the air. None of those techniques were successful. Moving closer, he raised the switch and slapped the hog on the rump a few times. Facing embarrassment in front of his future father-in-law, Greg continued to slap the hog and even tried encouragement (actually, begging is a better word), but with no luck. After a few more fruitless attempts with the hickory (and a few laughs) my dad reached into the back of his truck and picked up a short length of two-by-four, quietly walked up to the hog, hit him square on top of the head. The hog immediately stood up, shook his head a couple of times and hopped on the truck. Dad looked back at Greg and said something that I have found to be very profound. He said, "See son, you got to get the hog's attention before you can load him on the truck."

What a revelation! Motivation occurs in nature just as it does in the classroom. Of course we would never advocate the use of a two-by-four on a student. However, this story does underscore the fact that motivation is an individual event. Of the subjects in this reflection, each possessed a different stimulus required to be motivated to complete the task; that is, get on the truck. I think that it is safe to say that we can all identify what motivated the last pig, but what motivated the others? Was.it the desire to please, the need to leave the pen, or curiosity? It becomes incumbent upon the teacher not only to face the problem of student motivation with an understanding that motivation is diverse and individual, but to assess the stimulus required (what buttons to push) to move each student closer to the desired instructional outcomes. The idea of getting to know each student and thus determining motivational stimulus is admittedly critical to the establishment of the teacher-student relationship that allows teaching and learning to occur. Let us strive to motivate each one!

High Expectations

Interestingly enough, motivation in the classroom comes from the teacher's own beliefs about teaching and learning. The nature of the expectations teachers hold for his or her students exerts a powerful influence on classroom motivation (Raffini, 1993). To a large extent, students learn as their teachers expect them to learn (Stipec, 1988). School effectiveness research suggests that teacher expectations do have a self-fulfilling prophecy effect on student-achievement levels. Rosenthal and Jacobson's classic study *Pygmalion in the Classroom* (1968), while criticized for research flaws, nonetheless is an excellent example of this concept. Teachers in this study were led to believe that the students in their classes possessed exceptional academic talents. They were also led to believe that they were selected to teach the group of students because of their own outstanding teaching skills; in truth, neither was true. The expectations placed on the teachers to accomplish great feats and thus the expectations the teachers had of the students produced great results. The students far exceeded what was expected of them. Teachers, more often than not, get from students what they expect of them. If, as Wagar (1963) claims, "The ultimate function of a prophecy is not to tell the future but to make it" (p. 66), then each time teachers size up or size down a student they are, in effect, influencing this student's future behavior and achievements.

Expectations that teachers have of their students can without a doubt motivate them to succeed and achieve higher goals. In the current environment of accountability and the growing pressure to cover all the standards, teacher expectations seem to be doing just the opposite—gravitating toward the middle. By this we mean that the needs of both the low-achieving students and the high-achieving students are ignored to facilitate the "teaching of the standards." The "learn this and only this" approach is reinforced when students balk. This flawed motivational methodology is referred to by the authors as LDL (Learn Damnit Learn). LDL attempts to use a punitive approach to motivate students to meet teacher expectations. We must continue to reevaluate our assumptions about student learning. We should question the application of labels such as "underachiever," "overachiever," and "slow learner" as we continue to design classroom environments that are truly accepting of all students.

School Culture and Motivation

The reality of any place is what its people remember of it. What will this say for our schools? Another important factor to consider along with teacher expectations in regard to student motivation is that of school environment or culture. Schoolwide goals, policies, procedures, values, and beliefs can interact with classroom climate and practices to affirm or alter students' increasingly complex learning-related attitudes and beliefs.

Thus far in this book, we have defined "culture" as the racial, ethnic or socioeconomic background of the individual. In this context, however, the term "culture" means something quite different. It involves the heterogeneous cultures of the classrooms in a process that molds them into a singular culture. While the abandonment of individuality is frowned upon, in this case the value of each individual comes together to create a new culture accepted by all concerned, but without any diminishment of the individual properties contributed by its particular culture. Although no single definition of the term "school culture" has been established, there is general agreement that it involves deep patterns of values, beliefs, and traditions found over the course of the school's history (Deal & Peterson, 1998). Over time, groups tend to work out ways of getting along among themselves. They arrive at shared understandings of how, when, and where activities are to occur. Above all they specify the values, meanings, and purposes of these activities. In particular, thoughts and perceptions about what is worth striving for are a critical feature of any culture.

While the teacher serves as the catalyst for the culture in the classroom, the principal plays the role in initiating the vision for the culture of the whole school. The culture can be embodied and transformed through such channels as the school's shared values, heroes, rituals, ceremonies, stories, and cultural networks. If motivation and academic achievement are to be a definitive part of a school's culture, they must be communicated and celebrated in as many ways and forms as possible. It is the school principal that stands as the keeper of this process as it relates to the daily operation of the school.

School leaders enter the achievement equation both directly and indirectly. By exercising certain behaviors that facilitate learning, they directly control situational factors in which learning may occur. By shaping the school's instructional climate, thereby influencing the attitudes of teachers, students, parents, and the community at large toward education, they may increase both student and teacher motivation and indirectly impact learning gains.

As we have pointed out previously, all of these factors fully operationalize themselves in a perfect world. What then happens when the equilibrium that occurs naturally spins out of control? Have we created a "mandated" school culture that does not celebrate anything but conformity to a single score on a single assessment instrument? Has diversity in fact been discouraged and a singular mandate toward teaching and learning replaced the ideal motivating classroom? What have we done to teachers and how will this play itself out in the realization of a new order for American schools? How has the real role of the principal evolved from that of the facilitator of teaching and learning to that of the "task master" who oversees classroom instruction in a manner much like the supervision of an assembly line in a factory?

School climate and culture also shapes the environment for teaching and learning to occur inside the walls of the classroom. Following is the voice of one teacher regarding her classroom.

> You asked about the morale? Well the morale at my school is not so great. I try to be such a positive person and normally I am not a complainer. Many of those with whom I worked with in the past would always compliment me for being such a positive and encouraging coworker. Let me tell you, it is hard to continue when things at school are so low! My principal is not the least bit encouraging. In fact, at our last faculty meeting he announced that he didn't want to hire any more first-year teachers because in his words "they are too much of a hassle!" He even insinuated that our poor school test scores were our fault! I am one of seven first-year teachers at my school.
>
> Right now, I think he likes me and is pleased with my performance in the classroom but I know it's a matter of time before his wrath will be all over me like

white on rice! He yelled at [the teacher] in the cafeteria the other day because his class was too loud. With each day that passes I find that I do all that is humanly possible to avoid his evil eye. It's really sad; I go to great lengths just to avoid running into him.

It's not just the first-year teachers who have low morale, either. Most of the teachers in my school are thinking of transferring to another school or quitting altogether! Doesn't he know that we are real people with real feelings that should be treated better? I mean, I know I'm new and all but I think if the teachers were happy and were respected, they would be better teachers. I am not sure what can be done to improve the school atmosphere but I do know that something needs to happen and soon. I mean, it's really bad when no one wants to go to the faculty Christmas party! I think I am definitely in the category of I don't know if I can do this the rest of my life. Sad for a first-year teacher, don't you think!

Indeed! The culture of schooling today has driven many fine school leaders to this point, the point where they divert from what is right to what is expected. Due to her frustrations over this experience, this teacher left the profession after only two years of teaching. Our experience tells us that teaching, and its individual nature, is much like a herd of buffalo that stampeded across the prairie. Buffalo naturally spanned out and moved toward the task of pinning the settlers against the rim of the canyon, each moving at its own pace, along its own course, and in its own style. Even though each buffalo tackled the task differently, all buffalo were able to reach the same goal of pinning the settlers at the base of the canyon!

In today's schools, we regrettably see buffalo expected to stampede in a straight line, one behind the other, following the leader toward the task. In some cases principals are expecting all teachers to teach all children using the same methods, teaching specific subjects at the same time, at the same pace! If the task is to pin the settlers to the wall of the canyon, the diversified approach is more effective in meeting the objective than the single line; one after the other. While in the end both approaches at least partially meet the objective, the less orchestrated yields the chance of getting more of the settlers.

Principals and teachers need to have the courage to make the decisions that promote the moral dimensions of teaching, which are access to knowledge for all students, nurturing pedagogy, stewardship, and enculturating the young into a democracy (Goodlad, 1990). While we do not advocate civil disobedience, we do believe that for schools to make a difference today, taking the risk to develop leadership capable of undertaking the task of educating all children must resurface. With the current environment of accountability and all of the measures that come with this, it becomes increasingly unpopular to take this road. However, the wrong direction at this intersection may well result in an arrival at a destination that is not intended.

Capitalize on Students' Interests

Another characteristic often observed in teachers who are successful at motivating is the ability to determine what interests the students have and to capitalize on those interests to facilitate learning. Far too often, students who perform poorly in the classroom are labeled negatively, when in reality, they may be totally uninterested in what is being taught.

As we scan our society we see examples in play throughout the nation. In the U.S. Senate Hearing, "Crisis in Math and Science Education" (1999), Senator James Kohl, states:

> There are young people out there cutting raw cocaine with chemicals from the local hardware store. They are manufacturing new highs and new products by soaking marijuana in ever-changing agents, and each of these new drugs is more addictive, more deadly and less costly than the last. How is it that we have failed to tap that ingenuity, that sense of experimentation? How is it that these kids who can measure in grams and kilograms and can figure out complex monetary transactions cannot pass a simple math or chemistry test?

While we do not advocate motivation through the use of illegal means, this brings up a good point. Many of these students can do complex math and science problems when given the right motivation. With regard to communication skills, gang members can create, develop, and transmit a new written language understood only by members of the gang. Yet these same students are unwilling to learn to read and write in a typical classroom setting. Why? Can this chasm relate to the lack of contextual teaching in America's classrooms? Students are interested in drug dealing, as dealt within the above example, for obvious reasons, including financial remuneration and power. However, these same students may not be successful in schools due to subjection to disjointed nonrelated and isolated learning objectives. Educators must decide to spend time learning about their students' backgrounds, interests and, more importantly, lives. The time spent on the front end of the equation will produce results that are multiplied exponentially. One of the major criticisms of this concept is that activities based on student interests constitute a "total waste of instructional time." This feeling is exacerbated by the idea that there are more "standards" to be covered than time to cover them. Therefore, creative teaching and interest-based instruction are perceived as diversions from the "real" goal.

As educators we are making a major mistake if we fail to use the knowledge we have about our students, including their interests, to increase motivation in the classroom. Imagine a physician who would not ask you any questions or look at your medical folder in diagnosing an illness or a problem. Certainly we want our doctor to find out about our unique medical history and background. We seem to forget that teaching and learning are a two-way street, and that our success as teachers is proportionately related to the success of our students. Many times we treat students like common vessels that are merely receivers of knowledge. In other words, we say, "This is what you need to learn, memorize, and spit out for the test." However, the true art of teaching does require more assessment of the student outside the realm of the standards before the academic objectives can even be addressed. This assessment of needs and interests, we believe, may be underemphasized in teacher preparation programs. In our current educational environment, the regression to the average may be allowed, all for the sake of covering the material. Complacency by experienced teachers also contributes to the failure of a student's readiness to learn. Complacent teachers tend to feel that if things are going OK and that most of their students are doing alright, then why rock the boat? It's almost as if they treat teaching as just a job! Thankfully this is not true in the following narrative.

> Chad was, in many respects, a typical eighth grader. He had a tremendous need for acceptance by his peers, struggled with his roller-coaster emotions, and expressed (quite well, I might add) his lack of fondness for school. Like many students today, he saw no connection between what he wanted in life and what he was forced to do while in school. Chad had in fact become a classroom "problem" and had decided that his new mission in life was to be excluded from school. This pattern of misbehavior had been brewing for some time, yet he had moved from class to class and grade to grade. He was a source of frustration and aggravation for his teachers and could legitimately be characterized as a true pain in the classroom; in other words, every teacher's worst nightmare.
>
> As he entered the eighth grade even he was unprepared for what he was about to encounter. His new teachers had spent part of the summer planning and working together to prepare for the new crop of students. Each year the team tried to create, design, and implement new curriculum units for their students. This not only served as motivation for their students but kept them motivated and fresh as well. Chad's homeroom teacher, Mr. Granger, was also the team leader and had a reputation for being able to reach those hard-to-reach students. He had the belief that if his students failed, he somehow had failed as a teacher. He typically spent a lot of time at the beginning of the year getting to know his students, their interests, and basically what makes them tick. As classes began that year, Chad had begun his typical routine of noncooperative, empathetic, and increasingly disruptive behaviors. His full-blown adolescence made him even more obstinate than in the past.
>
> At the beginning of the school year Mr. Granger talked with Chad, and more importantly observed him and talked with not just his other academic teachers, but all of his teachers. He quickly observed that Chad performed quite well in his industrial technology class. In fact, he was a totally different student. He was very attentive, highly motivated, and very cooperative with the industrial technology teacher.
>
> Mr. Granger found out that there was no father at Chad's home and that his mother was working almost 12 hours a day just to make ends meet. To help his

mother, Chad, too, was working during the summers and on weekends with his uncle who was a homebuilder. Although Chad was young for the job, he was very adept at the tasks that were set before him. Mr. Granger recognized that the activities he was completing in his industrial technology class mirrored the work he completed with his uncle. Suddenly the way to motivate and engage Chad in the learning process was apparent.

With this information, Mr. Granger went back to the drawing board. Although he was a social studies teacher, Mr. Granger first went to the math teacher on his team. They were studying geometry and were just beginning to learn area and perimeter of various geometric shapes. Together they created a series of hands-on math lessons where they asked Chad to demonstrate for the class how to lay out a foundation for a house. It goes without saying that Chad very proudly demonstrated the concepts by laying the foundation of a house very much like the one he was currently building on the weekends. The math class went to the playground in the back of the school and used hands-on materials to mark off the house to scale. Eventually the math teacher did return to the handouts and exercises from the text for guided practice, but now Chad, a remedial math student, could help explain and tutor others in his class who were still having problems. And Chad experienced success, a new feeling for him.

Later in the year, Chad was building carbon dioxide race cars in his industrial technology class. In order to race the cars and win, the knowledge of aerodynamics was discussed and examined. Once again, Mr. Granger alerted Chad's physical science teacher and his motivation to learn was put to work. In language arts, the importance of communication and marketing and writing contracts for the sale of a house was brought to the forefront.

What does all this have to do with Mr. Granger, the social studies teacher? It's simple; Mr. Granger had to find a way for Chad to feel successful. No, Chad was not a straight A student and yes, at times he was still a handful, but Chad had experienced success and now he saw a connection between school and the world of work and he began to be empowered with his own ability to make something out of himself. It was this single teacher's understanding of what motivated Chad that created the doorway through which the other teachers passed. Through the collaboration of Chad's team of teachers, he was able to see the importance of doing well in school and how an education was essential to his success as a future homebuilder.

Unfortunately, Chad left the eighth grade very successful but went to the ninth grade without the same kind of caring, supportive, and nurturing teachers. He quickly lapsed back into his old routine of apathy, lack of effort, and even disruption. He soon became a statistic, a dropout.

If teachers could only understand that we teach students one at a time, each individually. We must work to find those activities that will move, motivate, and encourage our young people to succeed. If only we would do that, maybe we wouldn't have to lose all the Chads in the world.

Just as the story of Chad reveals, we must break away from the idea that students who do not respond to school are irresponsible and don't care. We must rock the boat! While no one could argue against the fact that students do have a responsibility to participate in the teaching and learning process, many of the approaches that have served educators well for decades (i.e., lecture, regimented, chalk and talk) just don't work well today. Times have changed, society has changed, and it is time for education to change too. It has often been said that if one were to fall asleep, much like Rip Van Winkle, and wake up 100 years later, the only thing that would probably look remotely the same would be our nation's schools! Why do we continue to do things the way we always have? Is it just because we always have? It's almost comical how in education we continue to whip the dead horse. The problem is not so much that education was done badly before; the problem is that we are trying to move our students into the Information Age where intellectual skills and training will be required of all citizens, not just a privileged few. In *Paradigm Lost: Reclaiming America's Educational Future*, author William G. Spady sees the current state of American education as "an iceberg adrift in a sea of ingrained habits, past practices and institutional inertia barely influenced by the winds of change and Information Age realities blowing on the top of its surface" (1999, p. 11). Are we just skimming the surface?

Tried and true ways of "doing" education may work fine for students who are willing and able to cope with a nonindividualized strategy for motivation. However, dismissing those not capable or even willing to cope as failures and not educable without looking for ways to reach them will not promote a society that bases its foundational beliefs on equity and access. One of the primary goals of education should be the desire to inspire all students to learn and become lifelong learners. A less comprehensive goal will deny citizens the opportunity, skills, and preparation necessary for the demands of tomorrow's world. We must spend time finding out about our students' interests and searching for methods to assist them in making the connection to context.

When you ask students to describe what it means to be a learner you will typically get responses such as, "doing better than most of my classmates," "making all A's," "turning in assignments on time." These are not the kind of answers one would want to hear. As long as we continue to allow students to define the learning process as winning and losing, we will continue to have students like Chad and many others who drop out or are pushed out by the system. This polarization of students into categories of "proficient" and "unsatisfactory" will perpetuate the order of American schooling as an elitist endeavor. When we fail to consider the interests of individual students, establish high expectations for them, and identify their needs, we are simply reducing school to a sport of beating the system and learning to play the game. If we continue to pursue this path, we will all be losers!

Managing Context

The next common characteristic of an effective classroom teacher's ability to motivate students may very well be the most difficult to implement, understand, and grasp. It is simply that great teachers manage context (class environment and conditions) and not students. Although this sounds easy enough, it has tremendous implications for teacher leadership in the classroom. The idea that the teacher is a leader (facilitator, instructional guide) is unfortunately foreign to many educators. In fact, the concept of teachers as leaders is not a widely accepted belief. Many teachers would even go to lengths to argue that the idea of teachers as leaders might actually be an oxymoron. Yet the true success of a given classroom in particular and our schools in general depends upon teachers who function as leaders.

Leadership exhibited by effective teachers is almost always based on the development of classroom relationships. Much of the current research regarding leadership invariably points to a number of characteristics that effective leaders exhibit while leading. These include vision, purpose, ownership, and empowerment. It is these foundational elements that allow leadership to emerge. So what does this say for the concept of teachers as leaders? Certainly the good ones are "in charge" of their classrooms, but is being "in charge" really leadership?

Most adults, not just students, tend to resent being managed by someone; however, they do tend to enjoy working with excellent leaders. Excellent leaders focus on creating and designing opportunities where people want to work hard, take risks, and work up to their potential. Poor leaders (people with whom others do not want to work, or follow) tend to do things in prescribed ways and with the use of time lines. While some required classroom activities do involve specific procedures and time lines, effective teachers provide choices, use hands-on activities, include less whole class/teacher-directed lessons, and encourage students to participate in class discussions. Effective teachers work toward student empowerment in their own learning to create a context-managed classroom.

In many respects this concept mirrors what the research tells us exists in a democratic classroom. Creating a democratic classroom environment means involving students on a regular basis in developmentally appropriate ways and in shared decision making, which increases their responsibility for helping make the classroom a good place to be and to learn.

In a classroom climate that is open and democratic, students are treated fairly and are free to express their opinions during discussion. Such a climate can prevail in classrooms that otherwise are traditional or innovative to varying degrees. The distinguishing and crucial factor is that in open, democratic classrooms students perceive their opinions to be solicited, accepted, and respected. It is in such classrooms that thinking is encouraged and nurtured. In fact, this idea of managing environment and conditions in effective classrooms lays the foundation for teachers to become excellent leaders in the instructional process. Effective teachers are excellent leaders in developing the environment that is most conducive to maximum student motivation and thus achievement.

Have you ever watched young children at play? Infants and young children are naturally propelled by curiosity, driven by an intense need to explore, interact with, and make sense of their environment. This confirms that indeed all children can learn. Unfortunately, as children grow their passion for learning frequently seems to shrink. Learning often becomes associated with drudgery instead of delight. As many as one in four students leave school before completing their school careers, and many more are physically present in the classroom but mentally absent. This fact has profound implications on American education and on American society in general. If we do not alter our present course, we will create a generation of citizens whose support for public schooling will be nonexistent. As stated before, the reality of any place is what its people remember of it. Again, we ask, what will this say about our schools and classrooms? Given these conditions it becomes even more critical that teacher leaders transform classrooms to be more fertile environments for self-motivated student learning.

To illustrate this idea, visualize moving a simple string from one place to another. No matter how hard you try, you just cannot push the string to where you want it to go. Students are like strings, too. It doesn't matter what position you take, what threats you make, or what bribes you offer, you cannot push a student to do something that he or she does not wish to do. If you are a parent, you know this is all too true. Have you ever gone shopping with middle school girls? We found out really quickly not to let our girls think that we liked or approved of an outfit. As soon as we tried to push them to make the selection we thought looked best on them, it was all over. They looked at the outfit as if it were disease ridden. If we bucked and bought the outfit anyway, you know what they did, they never wore it!

On the other hand, with great ease, you can pull a string in any direction that you want it to go. When we mange the environment, recognizing the value and contribution of each to a greater classroom whole and the context included therein, we as teachers need to develop the ability and the skills to pull the string, not push it. It is the pushing of the string that most demotivates it from moving in our desired direction. Let us strive not to push but to pull our students as we manage context to motivate!

We believe that the issue of teacher leadership is indeed critical to the reformation of schools, yet the current environment of schools hinders or even disallows this leadership to occur. For example, if vision is a component or characteristic of effective leadership, what vision can today's teachers have for their classrooms other than marking the standards and preparing for the state-mandated tests? To deviate from this requires risk and most certainly change. Only when vision can emanate from the leadership can true leadership occur. Effective teachers do lead and make countless decisions regarding their students each day. However, it is troubling that when the current school environment exists over time, it will in and of itself become the accepted culture, and concepts such as teacher leadership, student empowerment, and contextual teaching and learning will forever be replaced by the standards and the test. Teachers must emerge as the agents of change to create a new paradigm for education that is based on a locally developed vision of the future and on what students need to succeed, and shift to approaches that focus on collaboration, authentic contextual teaching and learning, and dynamic and effective strategies. According to William G. Spady, schools need to overcome a "bureaucratic-age culture, an industrial-age delivery system, and agriculture calendar and a feudal-age agenda" (1999, p. 9). It is the role of teacher leaders that will not only create a more motivational classroom and a more motivated student, but also set in motion the grassroots-level changes necessary to create this new paradigm for all educators.

The effective teacher must be able to assess the current status of each student with regard to needs. Many students are motivated; teachers have just not found the right combination to unlock their potential. Many times these students are labeled as unmotivated when they are simply struggling with their inner potential. This type of student can be difficult to deal with, especially for the novice teacher. To compound this problem, the student's frustration serves as a catalyst for further loss of confidence and lower achievement.

Haim Ginott (1972), noted educator, illustrates the frustration of this type of student with the following story.

> A drunk is staggering down the street and bumps into a stop sign. Dazed and disoriented, he steps back and advances in the same direction. Once again he runs into the sign. He retreats a few steps, waits, and then marches forward. Colliding with the sign again, he then resigns himself to failure saying, "there's no use, I am fenced in." (p. 239)

An underachieving student may be in a similar position. To her or him every obstacle is a stop sign of sorts that cannot be sidestepped. The teacher must understand that such students may not be motivated by praise because in their eyes they are already failures and believe that anyone who praises them is dishonest or insincere. Furthermore, students cannot be shamed into learning. Teachers who use phrases such as, "I know you can do it" or "You could make good grades if you applied yourself" rarely work as a singular source of motivation. Effective teachers understand that children can be invited into learning. They can be tempted but, for the most part, they cannot be shamed or manipulated into it. The current practice of labeling schools and students does not help either. Students who have a history of failure in schools are at a distinct disadvantage. Often, rather than fail, they choose to quit. "It is through achievement that academic self-confidence grows, and increased confidence in turn promotes achievement through inspiring further learning. In short, confidence and competence must increase together for either to prosper. When they do not grow apace, students are likely to suffer" (Covington & Beery, 1976, p. 5).

Reluctant, unmotivated students who have experienced failure enough times learn to expect no different. By managing the classroom environment, the teacher can create ways for this type of student to become reengaged by feeding both student intellect and student self-concept. The understanding that it is difficult for these students to learn without attention to the latter is much like having a great trip planned but no method of transportation to get to your destination.

Never, Ever Give Up

The following is a story told by a first-year, fifth grade teacher.

> As I read through each child's files the night before the first day of school, one child's stood out. His name is Tom. Tom had only been in Special Education for one year, but from what I read Tom had many problems for a long time. He came from a single-parent home, where he lived with his father. Over the past year in school he had tried to kill himself, he had hurt his classmates, kicked and cussed his teachers and told them many times how much he hated them. I knew right then that this was going to be a difficult year.
>
> On the first day, it was obvious that Tom did not want to be in my class. He wanted to be with what he called his "normal friends." I asked all my students on that first day to write their own mission statement. After crying and hitting himself on the head, he told me that he didn't expect anything of himself or of this school. He hated school and he most definitely hated me. The next weeks of school were filled with frustrations. He ran out the back of the school hoping to get run over. He hit his head

on a brick wall until his head began to bleed; he poked himself in the eye with a rock until it became red and swollen. He tried to tell everyone that I did it. He poked himself with lead hoping that it would kill him, and made machine guns out of paper pretending to kill all of us!

As a first-year teacher, I knew that this child needed so much more than what I could give him and I vowed right then to do all I could to help. It took much persuasion before I could convince Mental Health to get involved, and many conversations with his dad that the local "witch doctor's" herbs were not what he needed. I worried more and more about him and began to get up a little earlier each morning to say a special prayer just for Tom. After many meetings, phone calls, and accommodations, it finally started to happen.

I began to see Tom in a different light. I remember Tom was very upset one day for missing four problems on a math quiz. He said he could only miss three or he would get a "whoopin." I realized that Tom was scared of messing up and extremely scared of people being disappointed in him. Sometimes he just wouldn't do his work. He finally explained that when he does that, he chooses to fail so adults would believe that he was just a bad child, not that he couldn't do it. I decided that he just needed someone to realize that the mistakes he made were OK. He just needed someone to believe in him. I became more determined to let him know that he could do this work and that he was smart.

I started to handle Tom differently. Instead of marking his papers with an X for the wrong answers, I circled them and gave him another chance to fix his mistakes. I helped him get some new clothes and a book bag when his broke. I told him I believed in him and no matter what I would never give up. He had me for life.

Tom began to make some improvements. He made the honor roll and managed to go one whole week without having to visit the principal. He began to play at recess and even made a few friends. He still loses control sometimes but now he knows that it is not the best way to act and even apologized a couple of times for his outbreaks.

Tom moves on to middle school next year and I'll worry about him every day. He taught me far more than I did him this year. He taught me that teachers can make a difference as long as they are willing to fight for it.

Another concept in dealing with motivation stems from the authors' own experiences and observations. We believe that the most successful teachers never, ever give up! This is often described as a passion for the profession, a deep caring for all students, even a tenacious feeling of obligation to the profession. It is encapsulated in the notion that if the student fails, the teacher fails. Teaching and learning are viewed as equal components in this equation. These teachers are the ones who have the courage to do what is right by students even though they risk failure and isolation.

When delivered poorly or without regard to those previously stated concepts, teaching often doesn't consistently produce learning. The idea that when the students fail the teacher fails is not a popular concept among many teachers, especially among middle school and secondary school teachers.

Perhaps this is due to the predominant focus on content in training programs for teachers in secondary schools as opposed to the student-oriented approach for elementary teachers. While a natural assumption is that all teachers regardless of their grade levels possess the content background and knowledge, we believe that the first concern of every classroom should be to establish the environment for content to be delivered successfully. As teachers, we must remember that we teach students not subjects such as English, math or science.

This is a tough sell in a high-stakes testing environment, but to be truly effective teachers, we must view learning with a longer time frame. Great teachers seem to have almost a spiritual obligation for each student to succeed. Perhaps this is connected to their own need to achieve in a given task. Truly effective teachers never seem to give up on their students. Whatever the source, this part of the teacher's own personal philosophy or individual personality serves the students well with regard to student motivation.

Effective teachers often advise first-year teachers to continue to try again and again to find a way to reach each individual student. Time and again we reach the end of the school year feeling like nothing we did made a difference. We find out later that one kind word, one caring touch or one soft response can make an impact and give one student the courage to reach beyond the expectations of others and far exceed his or her potential. It is especially difficult for first-year teachers to feel as though they are making a difference with their students. Laurie, a first-year, first grade teacher shares one of those rare moments in a reflection.

> Sometimes the days and weeks at school seem to drag on forever in a constant struggle. We're all feeling a lot of pressure from the administration to bring up our test scores in order to can keep our federal funding. By the end of the year we are expected to have 100% of our students succeeding with flying colors. Each week we are expected to have perfect lesson plans turned in a week ahead of time. Sometimes I don't even know what I'm doing the next day, much less next week!
>
> But there are small reminders of why I continue do this day in and day out. The other day after school we were waiting for the last few buses to come. Alejandra looked up from her book and said, "You know, I'm the first reader in my family. And my daddy says that now I can be anything I want to be. I can even be a teacher because I'm learning so much in first grade." After hearing those words from one of my students it made all the negative things I was feeling about the teaching profession disappear. It made me ready to come back tomorrow and try again.

As we pull from our own experiences and backgrounds to work with our students, motivation still may not come easily, but like Laurie in the previous reflection, it usually does. And then we encounter (or will soon have the privilege of encountering) the class like no other. Affectionately, most educators call it "the class from hell." However, if one were to analyze the dynamics of this class one usually comes to the conclusion that only one or two students were the constant source of classroom disruptions, not the whole class. Yet the whole class became infamous due to lack of motivation to learn. The perceived lack of motivation created disequilibrium in the classroom, which altered our behavior as well as the behaviors of the motivated. In this type of situation, no one comes out a winner.

It becomes necessary for the teacher to assess these dynamic interactions within the class. This assessment is sometimes difficult due to the teacher's own methods of personal motivation. We have collected some informal data that lead the authors to believe that teachers' own patterns of motivation, including those that were developed when they themselves were students, have a foundational impact on classroom motivation techniques and understandings. We found that most teachers, especially elementary teachers, were intrinsically motivated and compliant students. Couple this with the fact that teachers tend to be more visual in their own learning style and you have a basic incongruence with the motivational needs and learning styles of most students who seem difficult to teach. It is our belief that if teachers are aware of and become proficient in this area of student needs, the characteristics of successful teachers outlined in this chapter can be more effectively implemented. Contextual teaching demands that this occur.

Many times, in teaching, we get bogged down with the obstacles that confront us. We have too many clerical chores to do, too many kids in our class, too many low achievers, too many parents to deal with, too many meetings to attend. The list goes on and on. These obstacles sometimes cause us to want to give up. It is easy to lose sight of our goals when everyday concerns crowd them out. However, if we can keep one goal in the forefront—to ensure learning for all students and to help them grow as wholesome, mature productive citizens— then the obstacles that we encounter along the way will take care of themselves. The obstacles don't go away, but they become easier to deal with when we focus our perspective by keeping our eye on the bigger picture. The following story is one that Geneal regularly shares with first-year teachers. It vividly illustrates the concept and power of never giving up.

> The story is one that has been told over and over again. There was once a little sandy-haired boy walking along the shores of the beach. Up ahead he noticed a section of the beach that was literally covered with hundreds of sand dollars. Knowing that they would soon die if they remained out of the water, he quickly began to toss the sand dollars back into the ocean. With each toss of a sand dollar, a life was saved. The young lad began to feel blissful and fulfilled. His arm grew tired but his determination to save each and every one did not die. He continued tirelessly until an elderly man

48 Teachers Teaching Teachers

approached. He watched the young lad for a short period and finally asked the boy just exactly what did he think he was doing? "Why, I'm saving the sand dollars, sir." The old man shook his head and said, "Why are you wasting your time doing that? Don't you know you can't save them all?" The sandy-haired boy stopped and thought for a minute and said "I guess you are right, sir." He then picked up another sand dollar and tossed it into the ocean and said, "But I just saved that one!"

In conclusion, we need to understand that student motivation to learn what we need and desire to teach is the single most critical factor to the success of our schools. Motivation is an individual act; what motivates one student may not motivate another. To be effective, motivation must address the needs and interests of our students. We must have high expectations of each and every one of them. Further, in motivating our students we must remember that we should manage context and not the students. And we must never, ever give up!

Schoolhouses can be elaborate "Taj Mahals" with every conceivable technology and material, yet without this single factor of motivated students the school is likely to fail. The concept of student motivation also affects the climate and interactions in classroom relationships. Motivation is difficult even in a perfect environment. But in the current condition of high-stakes testing, the road less traveled may be the direction that educators need to take. The other option is fraught with mundane worksheet-driven instruction, which may produce short-term gains but overall will be viewed by students as demotivating and in many cases not aligned with their interests or learning style preferences.

Aristotle said, "All men naturally desire to know." The obvious truth of his words is often lost when we work with children in our classrooms. We forget to take advantage of their natural desire to find things out. Instead we design lessons with the expressed or implied goals of force-feeding them with knowledge. Instead of students in pursuit of knowledge, we have the opposite—knowledge in pursuit of students. Learning is as natural as breathing and children have had lots of experience with the business of learning prior to entering school. We could take a tip from Marie Montessori in this regard. No matter what the age group, we should "prepare the environment" so that our students can access and assimilate knowledge in the most natural way possible. Only then will they learn the most and learn the best.

We work in a climate that is constantly changing. These changes are due to the ongoing mutation of society as a whole. Schools are, in fact, microcosms of the communities that they serve. These concepts force teachers to be professionals who work through changing environments and, in many respects, to "build the boat while you're in the water." It is through this aspect that the realization of a Holy Grail of student motivation does not exist. Rather, a professional educator who knows and cares for individual students; who truly believes that all children can learn; and never, ever gives up on students creates motivation in his or her classroom with each and every student, each and every year, and sometimes each and every minute of every day.

CHAPTER 3

Somewhere Between Church and Prison

Managing the Classroom Environment

Have you ever asked a veteran teacher what is wrong with the public schools of today? If you have, you probably heard narratives along the lines of students having bad attitudes, indigent home environments, an increasing lack of parental support, little or no respect for schools or teachers, and almost always without fail, a lack of discipline. As early as a 1987 report entitled *NEA Research/Gallup Opinion Polls: Public and K–12 Teacher Members*, teachers overwhelmingly stated their belief that parents and society are responsible for discipline problems occurring in schools. An alarming 64% of teachers polled stated that because of the problems at home, there is little that schools can do to bring about improved student behavior.

This scenario continues to play itself out year after year, Gallup poll after Gallup poll. Without control of the classroom, teachers cannot teach, and somebody has to be blamed for the problem. Are parents and society solely responsible for the lack of discipline in our classrooms? Is there not anything teachers can do to bring control back into our classrooms? As educators it is imperative that we ask and seek out the central factors in having a successful and well-run classroom. Are schools now a place where so much hopelessness exists that we can never reclaim the attainment of the American dream through a good education? Are students so difficult that order cannot prevail over chaos? Are we in a profession that does not learn from our own mistakes, or do we just continue to teach the way that it has always been done without any regard to the societal changes that surround us daily? Let's look at where we are and where we should be in order for schools and schooling to begin to make a difference in the lives of our youth. Undoubtedly, issues with classroom management are not new to the profession. As an example of where we are, here is a typical example of an induction teacher's thoughts.

> Going into teaching, I knew that discipline would be one of my biggest problems that first year. As a student teacher I was faced with some challenging students but in the back of my mind I always knew that I had my cooperating teacher to fall back on when all else failed. Let me just be honest with you; I was in no way prepared for the

reality of this challenge once my first year of teaching began with my own group of students.

When I began teaching I was (or at least I thought I was) well prepared. I had my rules posted, papers ready to distribute, and folders organized. My lesson plans were written. I told my class the first day that even though I was new to the school that I had taught before. (OK, so I'm stretching it a little by thinking that student teaching counts.) I certainly wasn't going to apologize and tell them that I was just a first-year teacher. I wanted them to think that I had experience so they wouldn't feel like they could take advantage of me. I also had decided that I didn't want to be as strict as my cooperating teacher. I wanted to give the kids a chance to behave on their own and naturally I wanted them to like me. My favorite teachers in school were those who were your friend and your teacher and I wanted to be that kind of teacher. On my first day I told my students I wanted to be their friend as well as their teacher. Funny, I thought it was that simple, just tell them you are their friend and their teacher.

This approach was actually working quite well until I met my last period class. It was a below-average eighth grade math class, 17 boys and 7 girls. As the semester progressed, I was able to gain control over my morning classes (for the most part) but all the good things that happened during the day could never counteract that last period class. The harder I tried the more they resisted. Most of the students disliked one another and there are just so many ways you can separate the "bad ones." I talked to everyone I thought could help me—my principal, the assistant principal, my mentor, and teachers who had had the same students the previous year. I tried everything they told me to do. Finally, I convinced myself that all beginning teachers have discipline problems. All I need is just more experience, right? It's not my fault that they are so bad. I began to believe this excuse; hell, it even became my motto. No matter what I did, that last period class just got worse and worse. I began to question why I even chose this profession. Why is it that kids don't care anymore? I would never have acted like that in class when I was their age. I loved school! I finally came up with the following conclusions: they don't pay me enough to put up with this and even though I love teaching, I'm not so sure this job is for me because I hate having to deal with discipline.

Without a doubt, some teachers probably think of classroom management, as the title of this chapter suggests, as somewhere between church and prison. When things are going well, they are really good, but when they are bad, they are really bad. How, as teachers, can we structure our classrooms to experience more of the good days and less of the bad ones? Is it even possible in today's ever-changing society to have classrooms where students are well behaved?

The debate over effective classroom management cannot be resolved to any degree until the question, "What is classroom management?" is addressed. For the most part, novice teachers, in fact most teachers, deem classroom management as synonymous with discipline. While management does involve the development and enforcement of rules, regulations, and procedures, it is much more complex than just discipline. If we look at classroom management as just discipline, do we in fact do more harm than good in establishing an environment that is conducive to teaching and learning? What social factors impact this critical sector of successful schooling? What are the key roles of the classroom stakeholders? Who are the classroom stakeholders? Are they just the teacher or are they teacher and students? What role, if any, does teacher leadership play in classroom management? What impact does the organizational culture of the school and community have on the efficient running of today's classrooms? We believe that these and other questions must be addressed in order to begin to understand the extremely complex relationships that occur in today's schools and classrooms.

Classroom Management is NOT…

Before we examine some of those questions, let's first look at what classroom management is not. First and foremost, classroom management is not discipline. The word "discipline" to most people has come to have the connotation of conformity, correction, and/or punishment. While many teachers believe that classroom discipline equates to classroom management, we contend that it does not. Punitive environments wrought with fear are classrooms that are not conducive to security and happiness, and certainly not to learning. We have all experienced classrooms that use coercion, control, and position authority to maintain order. Classrooms, where students are too afraid to ask questions for fear of being embarrassed, where participation of any kind is forbidden, where the teacher speaks while students listen, or where the teacher turns on the overhead and the students copy, are usually teeming with disruptive students. In settings such as these the instructional word of the day is *"quiet!"* The methodology is most certainly centered on lecture (likely on yellowed paper) and contains heaping helpings of drill and practice. What children in their right minds would freely go into a classroom such as this? Is it any wonder these classrooms are laden with unmanageable, unruly students?

Take a minute to think about the words "discipline" and "disciple." Is it a coincidence that both words have a common root? While discipline conjures visions of correction or punishment, the word "disciple" translates to "follower or learner who grasps the teaching of the leader." No organization flourishes in chaos and anarchy, and classrooms are no exception. Organizations cannot maximize their potential with punitive rule. Just look at the historical outcomes of a dictatorship. While the regime may flourish for a short time, it is always short-lived. Perhaps classrooms should combine the words "discipline" and "disciple" to create a framework of an environment where there is structure, yet the participants willingly follow the direction of the leader.

Second, classroom management is not a one-sided creation of the teacher. No matter how well thought out and user-friendly, the one-sided approach to discipline is not successful in terms of effective classroom management. There are several reasons why this is true. All teachers desire for their students to learn and do well. Where the teacher errs is that in most situations the system in place is reflective of what the teacher needs and wishes to execute. It is also based on the teacher's own behaviors and memories of his or her days as a student. Are you beginning to see why this approach is flawed? Like the teacher in the example mentioned previously, most teachers loved school, behaved in school, and were academically successful. But are these the type of students who present challenges in our classrooms today? Without fail, the answer to this question is a resounding no. With the changes occurring in our citizenry, schools have become very diverse environments. Yet many times teachers establish management plans that force this diversity to conform to something that is foreign and unknown to their background and culture. Teachers push students to act, believe, and perform like them instead of recognizing and capitalizing on their differences and seeing these differences as strengths.

Another flaw of control-type plans of teaching is that no one likes to be managed. Control really is just an illusion. This alludes to a student's loss of power and control, being left with no voice or choice regarding classroom proceedings. Instead of studying the possibilities, teachers seem to gravitate to what they know, all the while failing to maximize the potential of the students and thus continuing to disenfranchise those who do not comply. Many times this is done following the war cry of accountability through higher standards. In fact, it is this approach that lessens the probability that true changes in cognition within all members of the classrooms will occur. It is troubling that a new generation of teachers is being created, teachers who are cultured into the current system of American schooling rarely or never having seen the beauty of reaching that elusive learner, yet understanding too well the importance of labeling achievement and consequently students, classrooms, schools, and communities. One has only to pick up any newspaper or listen to any radio or television broadcast to substantiate this premise.

Finally, classroom management is not an environment in which everybody is happy and empowered and yet no teaching or learning occurs. Many times while working with novice teachers we hear the statement, "I don't want my students to think I'm mean; I want them to like me." Perhaps this concept revolves around the fact that most novice teachers are only 21 or 22 years old, and like their students, possess the strong pervasive human need to be accepted by the group. Often young teachers make decisions based on this need, which leads to disruptive outbursts and lack of control in the classroom. If this is the case it could transcend the need to be the adult in the classroom setting. What a concept! The teacher needs to belong to the classroom community and many disruptions in the classroom often revolve around the students' feeling of not belonging. Is human nature no different regardless of the age or status of the participants or is the complexity of this fragile engagement simply a relationship that is fulfilling to all members of the group?

Classroom Management IS…

While it is easier to assemble global examples of what classroom management is not, probably due to the experiences learned in failure, it is very difficult to say specifically what classroom management is. Perhaps this is due to the very diverse combinations of variables that come together in places we call schools. These variables include teacher attitude and background, school culture, classroom culture, ethnic and gender makeup, academic levels and abilities, subjects taught, and the list continues. It is easy to see that what constitutes good classroom organization and subsequently well-ordered learning environments can in fact vary from school to school and indeed from classroom to classroom. However, the authors believe that there are some necessary basic tenants that exist at the foundational level in these successful classrooms and schools.

If teachers are looking for a foolproof discipline system, they can be assured that they will never find it; it is much like the elusive search for the key to motivation. As each new class arrives in the classroom year after year, the management system must change to meet the diverse needs of the population the teachers are serving. The plan must be developed based on the needs of the students, their unique abilities and talents, and what it is that the teachers hope to accomplish. Discipline plans should not be viewed as charters, laws or theorems; they should simply serve as guidelines or a compass for the classroom. It has often been said and is all too true that with classroom management, if you fail to plan, you plan to fail. We must have some sort of plan in mind to be effective in the classroom. A simple example of this would be Geneal's teaching summer school in 2002 for 19 days to 14 second-grade students. During this very short time period, the name of the game was "monitor and adjust." One of the beauties about public school teaching is that each day is a new day; if it didn't work today, then tomorrow is a new day and one can attempt something different in the morning. Within that short period of time in summer school, four management plans were used. The first plan was teacher directed and had to be changed after only one day. It was a total disaster and a testament to the reality that it had not been based on the needs and interests of Geneal's students. After the first plan failed, subsequent plans evolved with the assistance of all participants in the class. Nineteen days and four management plans later, a working management system for the class had emerged.

Effective teachers must have a vision like that of the CEO of any organization. They need to be able to transmit the vision to their students and manage the class. Much of what it takes to manage a classroom occurs long before the students first walk through the door. For example, ask, How are you planning to arrange your physical space and organize student materials, work areas, and record keeping? What plan do you have for the many routine procedures (turning in completed work, sharpening pencils, morning routines, transitions, etc.) that will occur hundreds of times each day? The devil is in the details when it comes to classroom management. Managing a class entails making many decisions and it requires exceptional organizational skills. Procedures must be established and practiced for the classroom to function properly. In order for all students to be able to work effectively, the environment must be conducive to learning. When the environment is not conducive to learning, discipline problems occur. The book, *The First Days of School* is a good resource for planning and organizing the beginning of the year, especially for novice teachers (Wong & Wong, 1995).

To foster student involvement and cooperation in the classroom, effective teachers use a variety of strategies and methodologies to engage students in the lesson. When students are actively engaged in interesting, relevant learning activities, they are less likely to cause discipline problems. Often management problems are related to instructional problems; therefore, it is important to plan lessons that are in tune with desired learning outcomes. Still, at no point should management issues take precedence over the creation of meaningful instruction. The current brain research on how children learn shows that the strategies that we know to be the most effective are often those that are at risk for creating "ordered chaos" in the classroom. It is this "ordered chaos" that presents the most challenges to teachers who believe that for learning to occur students must be totally under control. Effective teachers are proactive in recognizing these challenges with engaging lessons that are well prepared and created to allow for a well-run, yet motivating classroom in which quiet is not the operative word.

Research validates that the most effective schools are those that have a well-ordered environment with high academic expectations. In the classroom, as the teacher, you want to establish a plan that will minimize classroom interruptions and maximize learning. It is the teacher who is primarily responsible for creating this environment. How exactly does one go about creating this? Without a doubt numerous books, papers, and articles have been written that supposedly guarantee the reader a cure-all to the classroom woes and challenges when it comes to managing the class. Discipline plans range from teacher-centered approaches to student-centered approaches; examples are William Glasser's *Discipline Without Tears*, Lee Canter's *Assertive Discipline*, Linda Albert's *A Teacher's Guide to Cooperative Discipline*, and many more too numerous to list. In a teacher-centered approach, the teacher's needs prevail. Methods of extrinsic control are used and it is the teacher who is the authority. All students are generally treated one way and the teacher's goal is compliance. In a student-centered approach, however, the teacher-student relationship is paramount. The authors feel this model is democracy in action; it is a responsibility model that fosters critical thinking by teaching students to make responsible choices. The student-centered approach allows students to feel more like "citizens" of classrooms and less like "tourists" by sharing leadership with students and giving them jobs of responsibility (Fielstein & Phelps, 2001). Beginning teachers usually use more of a teacher-centered approach early in their career. Where many fail is that they never turn the classroom into a place where the child-centered philosophy of management perseveres.

So just what is effective classroom management? First and foremost, effective classroom management is the establishment of positive relationships within the classroom and among and between the inhabitants of the classroom. This concept was discussed at length in chapter 1 and will appear in several other sections of this book. Why? Well, we firmly believe that this is the single factor that will set the environment for student and teacher success and satisfaction. Conversely, if the relationship development is negative, the system, school, classroom, and their respective participants are almost always doomed to failure, at least in the long run. Short-term superficial successes can be achieved through cohesive means but these are almost always short-lived.

One of the critical factors of successful relationship development in today's classrooms is the ability of the teacher to effectively model positive functioning behaviors. What the teacher does may, in fact, be more important than what he or she says. Trust must be developed not only between the class and the teacher but also between the students themselves. For the classroom to function effectively, these factors must be present. The role of the teacher in this scenario becomes more facilitative than directive with regard to assisting and encouraging diverse students to a level of trust and open communication. The following is an account of a first-year teacher.

This month has been challenging to say the least. I have had to learn fast. The more knowledge and experience I attain, the more knowledge and experience I realize I need to be successful as an educator. I never knew there was so much to learn about teaching. I am consistently a day behind and a dollar short. I never thought teaching would be easy. My husband is an elementary school principal. What I didn't expect is that teaching is a position that requires an overwhelming amount of time for the beginning teacher. I have had several teachers to watch and learn from. I have realized that teaching is more of a calling than a career choice. Few people would take my job, turn it into a career they love, and deal with difficult kids all day long for the salary teachers make, especially first-year teachers. I love my students. Although some have literally brought me to tears, there is a deep concern I have for their learning and well-being.

I am learning new ways daily to manage my classroom while increasing interest in my subject areas; however, I am limited to the amount of time I can spend on each objective. I just can't seem to get it all done. I feel like a failure in so many ways. I could be a better teacher if I had 48 hours in one day. I can see so many possibilities, but the reality of what I am able to do leaves me frustrated and with feelings of failure. I especially felt failure on two different days this past week. Let me share them with you.

I was in science class one day watching a film that a colleague of mine had raved about. I planned to view the video with my next science class on Wednesday. When Wednesday arrived I failed to remember that another teacher had asked for the room I was set up in. (Remember, I'm a floater.) Her class came to the door and I was caught by surprise. I quickly learned that tech prep students do not adjust to sudden change very well. I walked the students to her empty room and proceeded with the video. Since I was unprepared for the change, the students sat with whomever they desired while I adjusted to the move and got everything set up. What should not have been a surprise was a very disruptive class that no longer desired to pay attention or watch the video. I was forced to stop the movie and attempt to gain control of a few students who were talking. The rest of the class period was spent in contest, with no apparent winner.

The second challenge was when I caught a girl stealing in my class. She had the evidence in her book bag. She is often talkative and has little self-discipline. She is usually in ISS (in-school suspension) so I do not have to deal with her constant disruptions. She made a scene when I confronted her about the object and said offensive words that really hurt. I haven't yet got the thick skin that I guess you need to teach high school students. I understand the disadvantages that she, as well as others, may face at home. Nonetheless, outbursts of this type of behavior become discouraging and feelings of failure result. Thank you for allowing me to share my feelings.

Time appears to be a critical factor for this novice teacher; time she hasn't taken to establish working relationships with her students, and time she feels she can't afford to take for fear of getting behind her colleagues in covering the curriculum. The passion she feels for the profession and her students is present, yet the management issues were too overwhelming for her to conquer, and she left teaching halfway through the first year. Unfortunately, this is a recurring theme for those entering the profession.

A second way to achieve classroom management is to make sure that the expectations established within the classroom are clear to everybody. One of the pitfalls of the novice teacher (and some seasoned veterans) is to assume that the students understand just what is expected of them regarding behavioral and procedural events in the classroom. Just because the teacher understands what he or she means does not mean that the students also understand. Teachers, in order to overcome this hurdle, must take an approach that is usually different from what is taught in education preparation programs and from what they learn from their mentor teachers in most schools today. The simple task of developing a list of rules and consequences coupled with procedures will not guarantee student compliance. The authors quickly say that rules, consequences, and procedures are necessary to a well-ordered learning environment. However, clear expectations require student involvement in the development and implementation of these rules of conduct and also require that there is a conscientious effort on the part of the teacher to provide opportunities for students to revisit and be reminded of the expectations established for their classrooms.

Third, classrooms that are well managed will almost always contain student choices. These choices include both instruction and, more importantly, choices on the role students can play in a broader context of their school life. Students are not just "small adults." The authors believe that teaching choice and connecting the choice to personal responsibility is almost a moral obligation that schools have in a larger sense in preparing the next generation of democratic citizenry. All the same, there are practical reasons why we should give students choices and allow them opportunities to make decisions. First, we are more likely to get students to do what we want in the end if we allow choices and some personal responsibility in those choices. Second, choice promotes compliance and thus minimizes misbehaviors. Finally, letting students choose brings them to a level of self-discipline. By this we mean that the desired behavior will be carried out when no adults are watching.

While we do not advocate that total control of the classroom be placed in an environment of student choice, we do believe that successful classroom management includes opportunities for students to participate in their own destiny within the classroom. Without a doubt, this requires a special classroom relationship and a very skillful teacher.

Next, effective classrooms have a teacher that understands his or her power sources and how to best decide when and what kind of power to use. This is an interesting concept and one that is at best remotely addressed in teacher training. If a student comes to the point of frustration to say, "You can't make me," in essence the student is right. So how does the teacher deal with this aspect of classroom management? First, we believe that the teacher must understand the difference between power and control. As stated earlier, students should be given choices; however, this can only occur when the teacher understands power, control, and the sources of these two concepts (Jensen & Kiley, 2000).

Earlier in this chapter we said that control is an illusion, but teacher power is not. Teachers get their power from four basic sources: (1) referent power—the students view the teacher as a person; (2) expert power—the teacher has special knowledge; (3) legitimate power—the teacher has legal authority; and (4) reward/coercive power—the teacher can reward or punish. In effective classrooms there is a balance between these power sources, with heavy emphasis on referent and expert power. The use of referent power is minimal in the need for student control and communicates caring to the students. The use of expert power is also minimal in the need for student control and the students recognize the expertise that the teacher possesses and values it. The use of legitimate power is moderate in the need for student control and assumes that the students have a respect for the legal authority. The effectiveness of this approach to gain control of our classrooms is waning due to many societal changes that we face in schools. Finally, reward/coercive power requires a high level of student control and places the students in a position to believe that all the teacher knows about them is what they like and dislike, in order to dispense rewards and punishment.

It is disconcerting that we see many classrooms operating on a regular basis using predominately legitimate and reward/coercive power. After all, it's easier and requires less work on the part of the teacher. However, it will not provide long-term student success because it will not move the student toward self-disciplined, intrinsically motivated levels of learning participants. Effective management of the classroom should move students from teacher-monitored to self-monitored to self-controlled in the same manner that we would move students through a scope and sequence of any curriculum area.

Finally, in establishing classroom management, the curriculum must be relevant to the students (or at least presented in a relevant manner). This is perhaps the most illusive of any of the foundational elements of effective classroom management, largely because of the narrowly prescribed curriculum standards and all the false assumptions about students and learning contained therein.

This environment of high-stakes testing that we see infesting schools across the country has forced many teachers to finely develop a pedagogical approach to teaching affectionately referred to as DSK, or "drill, skill, and kill." This singular, one-size-fits-all approach to teaching runs headlong into a student population that is growing in diversity, not only culturally but also in learning styles and preferences among these students. It is no wonder that teachers find themselves in situations where their classrooms are out of control. Effective classroom managers take even standards-driven curriculum and contextualize it using relevant methodology such as service learning, cooperative learning, and project-based instruction and students then develop ownership with regard to their own learning.

Stumbling Blocks to Effective Classroom Management

So if we know what elements are contained in effective classroom management, why do we not just package the program, standardize the training, and implement the entire plan and see that all those unruly, unproductive classrooms in our schools disappear forever? Well, the authors believe that one of the beauties of our profession lies in its diversity; diversity not only in our students, but also in what we as educators bring to the classroom. These differences create a perfect environment within which we should be able to celebrate and teach children the strength of their differences, yet we find ourselves constantly being forced to standardize everything from curriculum to behavior to methodology, all for the sake of the results. The reality of this creates stumbling blocks to effective classroom management. We present these stumbling blocks as they influence student behavior, as well as focusing on institutional issues that have impact classroom management.

One way of understanding children's unproductive school behavior is to argue that this behavior is linked to a result of children not having their basic needs met within the environment where these behaviors occur. The authors agree strongly that it is the teacher who controls many of the factors that will influence children's behaviors. The following is a reflection from Jennifer Mills, a first-year teacher who learned this very important lesson early in her career.

> Until this year, I was unaware of just how sheltered my life has been. I grew up in a home that was stable in every respect. I have two loving parents who taught me the value of family, friends, and loving relationships. I have two wonderful, overprotective brothers and a very close extended family. My family has lived in the same city for nineteen years now, providing me with a very stable public education. I attended a private liberal arts college with a prestigious reputation, where I met many wonderful people and received a solid education. Although I am not claiming to have had a

picture-perfect life, I have indeed been guided, loved, and sheltered. My first year as a teacher opened my eyes to a completely different world!

I currently teach at a rural elementary school that is comprised of a very transient student population from a wide range of socioeconomic levels. It is designated as a Title I school, which is a federal program that provides funds to enhance academic opportunities for students needing additional academic assistance. Thus, our school population largely consists of very needy children, both academically and emotionally. The students in my class are no exception. I have heard shocking, first-hand accounts of neglect, abuse, murder, and violence through the innocent mouths of six-year-old children. Two students' life experiences in particular have deeply touched my heart.

Ray is a very happy, well-behaved student who actively and excitedly participates in classroom activities. However, he is habitually late to school, very irresponsible with his belongings, and is not as mature as the other students. I quickly guessed that his home life was not one to be desired, but I had no substantial evidence upon which to base my assumption. Then, early in October, Ray came to school complaining of a stomach ache. I did not think much of it at first and simply urged him to get a drink of water (the cure-all for most first grade ailments). When his complaining continued, I took him aside and asked him about it. Ray said that his dad had "punched him in the stomach" that morning. Alarmed, I questioned him further about the incident, and Ray revealed that his dad "punched him in the face, threw him on the bed, and then punched him in the stomach." Indeed, when the school nurse examined him, she noticed swelling in Ray's stomach, and he recounted for her the exact scenario that he had told me.

As the school year continued, Ray's tardiness increasingly became a problem. He was missing important material—material that he of all students needed not to miss. He was struggling greatly academically, but every effort that I made to contact his mother was to no avail. They changed residences often, so I was left with several disconnected numbers throughout the year. On the few occasions that I was able to speak with her, she was very short and anxious to get off the telephone. She seemed to avoid me at any cost. One morning when I approached Ray, his excuse for being late was that he was "playing a game." When I tried to explain to him that "playing a game" was not an excuse for being late to school, he desperately replied, "But my mom wouldn't get up. I kept trying to wake her up, but she wouldn't get up! She just rolled over and went 'ughhhh!' It was not until that moment that I realized just how much responsibility was being placed on this six-year-old child. Not only is he expected to wake himself up every morning, but he is responsible for getting himself dressed, fed, and on the bus. When he misses the bus (which is often the case) he is forced to beg someone to get out of bed and take him to school.

John's personality is drastically different from Ray's. He is painfully shy and reveals little to no information about his home life, interests, likes or dislikes. Considering the fact that I am constantly bombarded with stories and personal information throughout the day from my other students, I found it very surprising that John could not find anything that he wanted to share with me. In fact, during the first week of school, he crouched in the hallway and cried every morning, refusing to come to my class. John shies away from any attempt that either I or the other students make to touch or show affection toward him. It seems to be physically painful for him to participate in our daily "Share Square." "Share Square" is a time set aside to allow students to share something about themselves and their experiences. He does not want to participate in class games, plays or productions. He sits alone most days during lunch and plays alone at recess. When I investigated this situation, I discovered that John was born to a mother who abused cocaine while she was pregnant. She lost custody of him when the court found her guilty of neglect, and his grandmother adopted him.

The school year went on, and although John clearly became more comfortable in the classroom and opened up a little, he still remained highly reserved and extremely sensitive. One Friday in late April, I noticed that John was coughing a little throughout the day. I encouraged him to get water, but the coughing seemed to be nothing major. At lunch, John approached me and asked if he could go see the nurse because he was coughing. John rarely complains. In fact, I can only remember one other time that he mentioned that something was bothering him. I knew that he truly did not feel well, and sent him to the nurse. His grandmother was contacted, he returned to class, packed up, and went home. On Monday, he came to school, and I immediately noticed that he was still coughing. It worsened throughout the day, and I sent him to the nurse again. Shortly after, the nurse came down to my room and informed me that John has asthma, but that he had been using a family member's inhaler because no one at home would buy him one of his own. When John's uncle came to pick him up, John was gasping for air, choking on every breath. Seemingly unfazed, his uncle attempted to slip out so as not to be confronted about the alarming situation. However, the nurse cornered him and informed him that John was not to come back to school without an inhaler of his own. The next day, John came to school with his own inhaler.

Shortly after the asthma incident, I was confronted with some alarming information concerning John's background. I discovered that John's mother is currently serving a 30-year sentence in jail for multiple offenses including armed robbery, possession of a weapon, and fleeing from the police. She has currently served 5 of her 30 years. When I discovered this, my heart ached for John. Have these memories from John's early childhood stuck with him, causing him to avoid any type of relationship? Has he refused to trust anyone for fear that they will abandon or betray him?

Ray and John are two children who have opened my eyes to an unfamiliar world where love, trust, acceptance, and protection are not guaranteed for a child. My life and experiences stand in stark contrast to those of most of the children that I currently teach. Each of my students has impacted my life in a unique way. Each one has taught me something about either myself or life in general. I learned that not every student comes from a warm, loving family like the one that I grew up in. I learned that some kids enjoy school more than they enjoy life at home. I learned that some kids have more responsibility at the age of 6 than most kids have at the age of 15. I learned that some children dread school holidays and summer vacation because they have to spend them at home. Finally, I learned that some things that a child receives at school, like love, acceptance, and a trusting atmosphere, are more important than the academic skills that they are expected to receive. I have indeed been a student myself this year, learning right alongside my babies.

Another theory of unproductive student behavior is to see it as just what it is—a skill deficit. Students who act out on the playground by being aggressive with their peers or speak out during instructional time may lack the necessary skills in understanding how to handle conflicts or how to behave in a social group. If this is the case, as educators we must create opportunities for our students to develop those skills. Our society is changing at such an alarming rate that the purpose of schooling as our forefathers intended it is changing to include many responsibilities and obligations that were once parental responsibilities. Many of the basic human needs that once were met in our homes now reside in our classrooms. Our students are coming to our schools from homes where the only solutions modeled for solving our problems or conflicts are those of a violent, negative nature. The role of teacher must evolve to meet these challenges that are present today in our classrooms. Are we preparing preservice teachers for this changing role? Are we addressing these issues with induction classes, or better yet, with our seasoned teachers in professional staff development?

Walter Doyle (1986) describes six features of classrooms that often add to the difficulty and complexity of managing a classroom. The first feature is that classrooms are multidimensional in that they are complex social systems where many things are going on at several different levels, both inside and outside the classroom. Advice often given to novice teachers is that they must have "eyes in the back of their heads." Teacher candidates are routinely asked to videotape their teaching and to observe not just their own teaching but also student reactions to their teaching. Common comments made by the teacher candidates about their teaching revolve around what the students were actually doing while they were teaching. "How could I have missed that?" "I never even knew they weren't paying attention." Simultaneity is a second feature of classrooms that creates difficulty. Not only does much activity occur in the classroom, but it also all occurs at the same time! Multitasking is a much-needed skill in managing a classroom. A student is upset and has just broken the point off his last pencil. While continuing to teach, the effective teacher would simply take away the broken pencil and give him a new one. This is not a time to stop teaching; just handle the problem and continue to teach. A third feature is unpredictability. Even with our best-laid plans, fully prepared lessons rarely go as planned. How can we predict a fire drill? How can we plan for the student who gets sick in the middle of a lesson or the new student who arrives halfway through the class period? "Monitor and adjust" has to be the law of the land with this feature.

Immediacy is another feature present in all classes that can lead to unmanageability. Teachers need to be able to respond to the unknown and to respond quickly. Because of the fast pace of the classroom, there is little time to stop and think. Teacher candidates working with veteran teachers will often ask them at the end of the day how they knew how to handle a particular situation. For those teachers who are unconsciously skilled, it is hard for them to put into words how it is that they know what to do; they just do. A fifth feature is publicness. Not only is it difficult for novice teachers to deal with scrutiny from their principal, peers, and parents; they also experience a general lack of privacy in the classroom. Students are spectators to a teacher's every word and action. In a teacher's dealing with one student concerning a particular behavior in class, the other students are witness to how he or she handles the situation. This in turn will affect future situations and relationships with other students. The last problematic feature of classrooms is history. The past influences the present and the future life in a classroom. The authors like to relate to this characteristic when teachers seem to have lost all control in their classroom. Students learn very quickly what makes a teacher tick; they remember how teachers will react in certain circumstances and they will often find all the right buttons to push. Once this occurs, it is very difficult, if not impossible, for the teacher to regain control of the classroom. History can serve to be an effective tool in managing the classroom if consistency is present. Consistency is critical if you expect history to work in your favor.

There are other factors that impact classroom management, some of which are out of the realm of teacher control. One of the most formidable is that of time. How long have we had a school year (for instructional delivery purposes) that averages around 180 days? This archaic idea can be a factor in all aspects of total school success, but has a specific impact on classroom management. If we need to develop relationships with our students in order for classrooms to work, then within the context of standards-driven curriculum and high-stakes testing there just isn't enough time for that luxury. How often do we read in the newspaper or hear on television how students in other countries are outscoring our students on standardized tests? Almost without fail, their school year is much longer in days than our school year. The general public and legislators scream for reform, accountability, and thus student achievement yet are the first to hold on to the current time structure of a school year. Perhaps the public sees changing the length of time children participate in schooling as an inconvenience to vacation schedules and other family events or they simply lack the understanding of the complexities of education and the impact of time on the success of these educational endeavors. Currently in South Carolina there is a bill before the General Assembly that would mandate a common starting date for all schools in all districts across South Carolina. This date would preferably occur after Labor Day in order to allow for a cheap labor force in the tourist industry and to lengthen the vacation period for families. Ironically, many school districts are opting to begin school on or around August 1 to allocate more teaching days prior to the state-mandated test, the Palmetto Achievement Challenge Test (PACT). Which agenda will the lawmakers opt for in this dilemma? Perhaps the lawmakers will look upon this dilemma as an economic issue. More school days equal longer teacher contracts and subsequently more money. These "supporters" of school reform see schools as existing solely for economic growth and gains. Many of them believe that student achievement simply can be legislated. These mandates will result in students learning and teachers teaching more effectively. How sad that these ill-thought approaches will guarantee a social underclass of those who, for whatever reason, do not meet the standard.

Another factor that can derail even the most well-developed management plan is the curriculum. We have said before that the relevance of the curriculum is a key link to motivation on the part of the students and that it is a major factor in classroom management. So why mention it again? The authors of this book believe that creative, skilled, successful teachers can take even a narrowly focused, standards-driven curriculum and contextualize it to make relevant connections to their students. Focus should be on pedagogy and methodology to make this occur. The pressures of accountability force many teachers to abandon what is right for what is expedient. If the principal says, "We will use this program for teaching our students to read," then that is indeed what happens. Variation from that single, narrow-minded approach is met with responsibility that many teachers just do not want to accept even though professional judgment indicates the existence of flaws in the system. The battle is just too hard for them to fight, the system wins, and the students lose.

For educators to overcome this obstacle we must develop and exert leadership beginning at the classroom level. We believe that teacher educators must assist by changing their role as conveyors of content, theory, and methods to true collaboration within school districts and classrooms. Only when we are all working together on the same team with the same mission will reform of this nature occur. This collaboration can only assist in the change necessary for our schools to truly meet the needs of all of our students.

Another interesting issue that can appear as a stumbling block to effective classroom management is simply called finality. By this we mean that most teachers are trained to have a plan in place, complete with routines and procedures, when the students arrive on the first day. Certainly, the authors do not question this practice but agree wholeheartedly with the concept. However, most teachers are not taught that these plans are not final. Assessment of the classroom and thus the effectiveness of the management plan is probably the most important assessment in which a successful teacher engages. Students change, relationships change and develop over time, and any manner of other variables change, all impacting the plan that is in place to create a learning environment. Without constant reassessment of the plan it will not yield the fruitful results as were originally intended.

Our own personalities and personal characteristics can create issues and be stumbling blocks that affect our success in creating an effective classroom. We said in chapter 2 that the majority of teachers in today's classrooms, especially at the elementary level, have a common set of characteristics. These include a history of compliance in their own student days, they were intrinsically motivated, they demonstrated a predominance of a visual learning style, and for the most part, they had positive personal experiences as students themselves. The kinds of students just described don't create problems in the classroom. In fact, the authors of this book believe that there are fewer and fewer of these kinds of students attending schools today. These facts demand an increased emphasis on both theoretical concepts and increased clinical experiences offered as part of the preservice teacher's course of study. This is especially important with regard to the growing homogeneity of elementary teachers. These early experiences with schooling that occur in our elementary and early childhood classrooms in many respects set the tone for the future successes and failures for the students they will teach one day. Understanding the differences of students and having a theoretical and practical approach to deal with them helps to create an effective classroom where success occurs and can be replicated for the students as they progress through the education system.

Along with this concept is the fact that while America's teaching force may be growing more homogeneous, the students in the classroom certainly are not. We are facing these changes at an alarming rate. Our family structure is changing to the degree that families with both natural parents are now the minority. The ethnic and racial makeup of a classroom is also changing. The rapid rise of Hispanic students and students for whom English is a second language is becoming a formidable factor in the diversity in our classrooms.

All of these changes in our student demographic profile need to be addressed. For the most part, teacher education programs are addressing diversity in teacher preparation programs. However, what happens when the growing diversity runs headlong with high-stakes testing is another matter altogether. How does one hold a sixth-grade Hispanic student accountable for the sixth grade standards in reading and math when he or she doesn't speak, read, or write in the language of the test? Yet that is exactly what is happening. Then what happens? We tend to label him or her or relegate him or her to a special education class, or worse, fail to do anything to meet his or her needs.

So what does all of this have to do with management of the classroom? Remember, earlier we said that management was not discipline. If we see the characteristics of students in our classroom as challenges to the management of the classroom and focus on management as has been defined in this chapter as the vehicle of student and teacher success, then we begin to make progress in helping to create a classroom in which all students can maximize their potential.

Conclusion

In this chapter the authors have discussed what classroom management is and is not and have pointed out institutional realities that serve as stumbling blocks to having and executing an effective classroom management plan. However, this is an extremely complex topic and merits continuous assessment of the efficacy as measured by the overall achievement of the students.

Known as the "father of classroom management" by many in the field, Jacob Kounin (1970) was one of the first to conduct a study on what effective teachers do when it comes to managing a classroom. After hundreds of classroom observations he was able to identify preventive approaches to managing classrooms. One characteristic Kounin discovered that effective classroom teachers have was "with-it-ness." Teachers who are "with-it" are able to anticipate potential problems and plan accordingly. "With-it" teachers know at all times what is going on in their classroom. They have the teacher look. Much of this type of management is nonverbal. In the early stages of Geneal's teaching career, Greg often said that I could direct my classroom with my eyebrows and a few hand signals. Kounin found that effective teachers possessed the ability to do just that, as well as to multitask; in other words, they could address a question from the office while passing out papers for the next assignment and while checking students' folders for the previous night's homework.

Classrooms are busy places with many things occurring simultaneously. One of the most difficult areas for new teachers to grasp in the classroom, which falls hand and hand with with-it-ness is pacing. How long does one give a student to complete an assignment before moving on? How does one transition from one activity to the next? How does one handle the students who finish early? Effective teachers are keenly aware of all of these issues and able to handle the momentum and flow of a typical classroom.

In addition to the momentum, flow, and multitasking environment in successful classrooms, teachers must also be aware of the culture, diversity, and personality of the class in order to maximize the student success opportunities that should occur within effective classrooms.

The authors of this book firmly believe that the successful classroom is permeated with the components of democratic and socially just principles. These play themselves out in both small and almost undetectable behaviors as well as in very obvious teacher-student interactions. In order for the classroom to work within the context of democracy, the teacher must:

- Have a clear sense of his or her own cultural and ethnic identities.

- Have high expectations for the success of all students (and the belief that all students can succeed).

- Be committed to achieving equity for all students and believe that schooling is capable of making a difference in the students' lives.

- Ensure that students are provided with an academically challenging curriculum that includes attention to the development of higher-level cognitive skills.

- Provide instruction that is relevant to the needs and interests of the students.

- Encourage parental and school community involvement in the education of students.

- Teach the culture of the school while maintaining the cultural differences of the individual.

These concepts, when in place, will provide a structure within which students will not need to be managed but rather coached, guided, and directed. The teacher in a democratic classroom acts as a facilitator of learning, not a simple conveyor of knowledge. When classrooms reach this level of productivity, the place we call school reaches a new level. It now becomes a place where students and teachers come together in a partnership, not an adversarial relationship, where both are intent on the success and satisfaction of the other. Indeed, this is how the place we call school should function!

CHAPTER 4

Is Anybody Listening?

Communication in the Classroom and Beyond

Recently upon listening to a group of induction teachers reflect on the trials and tribulations of only the fourth week of school, the authors of this book gained a better understanding of the significance and difficulties with regard to communication both in the classroom and beyond. As each novice teacher was sharing their challenges with the group it was obvious that they were well prepared with regard to their content knowledge for their particular classroom. Even though this was their first year of teaching, it appeared that their management plans were beginning to take shape and each had a good handle on the background and needs of the students who were in their classrooms. However, most were still experiencing difficulties with their first year of teaching. What exactly was at the root of their collective problems? Definitely many things were going right but something was also going wrong. What was it and could anything be done to prevent those issues from recurring in the future?

After continuing to ask questions and listening and making notes we were able to gather enough data to analyze the situation. It quickly became evident that there were definite communication problems occurring within and outside of their respective classrooms. The young teachers had left important issues with students, parents, and staff unrecognized, unresolved, and unanswered. When questioned as to how they went about communicating these concerns, responses from the young teachers varied. One who taught fifth grade said, "I told my students three times what to do in class. I just don't see how they could have missed those directions." Another said, "The students' parents know to call me if they have any questions about school. All the parents would have to do is to refer to the note that I sent home at the beginning of the year with their child." Sadly, one novice teacher said she had given up because she had tried three times to contact this particular parent and no one would return her calls. Our personal favorites were, "We just assumed that the note we sent home would actually make it there" and "Those lunch ladies are always looking and talking about me. I don't think they like me." Well, experience will tell you that assuming never works, especially in education. As stated in chapter 1, teaching is all about relationships, and that includes working with staff members, parents, and students. Plainly, the chasm that existed in each scenario occurred between the sender and the receiver. A clear communication feedback and direction loop had not been established between the parties involved. Our teachers assumed that the messages they sent were received and understood on all levels. In some cases, the novice teachers were not even aware of the unintended messages they were sending.

Effective teachers are successful because they hold productive and efficient communication skills. They understand that one of the keys to good communication is determined by the climate of the classroom. The climate affects and influences how they interact with your students, but more importantly, how students interact with the teachers. The climate determines the manner and degree to which the teacher exercises authority, shows warmth, provides support, encourages cooperation, and allows for independent judgment and choice. Interactions that occur between teachers and students are at the very heart and core of teaching. These interactions require effective communication skills. It was those interactions that were missing in the scenarios described at the beginning of this chapter. In classrooms where positive group dynamics exist, teachers and students are able to work toward a common goal; that is, learning. The power of what each individual perceives to be reality is what makes communication so intriguing, so rewarding, and yet so scary. Effective teachers understand this power; they understand the importance of communication.

Definition of Communication

The word "communicate" comes from the Latin word *communicare*, which means to make sense or make known. Let us define "communication" as the ability to share information with people and to understand what information and feelings are being conveyed. It is a social process the ultimate purpose of which is a common understanding among all participants. Communication can take on many forms. We communicate by speaking, writing, listening, and by observing people's body language. We communicate with others not only by what we say but also by how we say it. We've all been in situations where what we thought we said and how others perceived it were in total opposition to the original message that was intended. If you have children, a multitude of stories should come to mind to serve as an example. Greg and I have two daughters. I had difficulty getting pregnant with our first child and just assumed I would have the same difficulty with the second. Yet our second daughter was born a mere 16 months after the first! We often joked with our friends about the day we found out that we were expecting for the second time. We were definitely surprised and shocked, and not exactly ready for a second child. I had even gone to the trouble to buy a stuffed rabbit and had it on Greg's desk at school with a sign that read "the rabbit died." This time it was Greg who experienced morning sickness for six weeks. Our youngest has heard this story many times and always laughed and smiled as she listened to it. However, she interpreted it to mean that we didn't want her. By no means did we ever feel that way, but it was what she heard. It wasn't until she was 16 years old that we realized the depth of her hurt over this story, which to mom and dad was just a funny story. Perception plays an important role in the communication process. Your perception is your reality!

Communication is not just one event, either; it can take on many forms, including gestures, facial expressions, postures, spoken language, and written language. We can speak kind words, yet our body language can deliver a totally different message. Our facial expressions can communicate confidence and determination when our words convey the exact opposite. Perhaps it is the many different forms of communication that exist that cause our messages to often be misinterpreted.

In conjunction with using many forms of communication every day, one must also consider the complexity of the interaction that occurs between the communication techniques used by the sender and the techniques used by the receiver of the intended information. Caring interpersonal interactions are essential to meeting student needs. As stated in chapter 1, students will not care until they know that you care. The interaction and relationship between the sender and receiver must be one of mutual respect and genuine caring, and must be on solid ground. Often it is the misinterpretation of our messages and intent that occurs in and out of school that creates many of the difficulties experienced by teachers in today's classrooms, both young and old. Effective, efficient, and viable communication skills can alleviate much of these difficulties.

Teachers must recognize and take advantage of the important connection between home and school as it occurs in effective communication. Those of us who have been privileged enough to walk this earth for more than 40 years remember a different childhood than what is currently faced by our youth today. In our day, there was no cable television; you only had three channels if your family owned a TV at all. There was no *Sesame Street*, video games didn't even exist, and there were no computers or cell phones. The television shows almost always exuded the family values of the time, with a family consisting of two loving parents, two children, a nice large house with a white picket fence, and a family dog. Minorities were rarely seen on television and when they were, it was in a diminutive light. It was rare to witness a couple kissing. Only then it was just a peck on the cheek or lips. What a difference in what is experienced by the children of today!

In order for communication to be effective we must be sensitive to the cultural differences between the students and parents with whom we work on a daily basis. Without placing communication into a realistic sociocultural context, these complexities most certainly will not be realized and acted on by the teachers. Our friends, who are authors, Joe Kincheloe and Shirley Steinberg, have developed the concept of "kinderculture," which is a complex look at childhood and the bombardment of children by both historical and realistic perspectives. It also addresses the multitude of stimuli present in today's world. Their work in this area has encouraged research, debate, and progress toward the understanding of childhood, and it also has implications for analyzing adult behaviors and connecting them to the future of democracy. The authors of this book believe that this concept of "kinderculture" has great implications with regard to effective communication in both the school and the home. We often experience confusion while working with several different norms, especially when it comes to understanding and communicating to the parties involved. A simple illustration of this concept is as follows. Asking Hispanic students to make eye contact during a conversation is in direct contrast to their cultural norms. Cultural issues in regard to communication will be discussed later in the chapter.

Does the concept of the current conditions that realistically exist in children's environments strike a sharp chord of incongruence with the curriculums and methodologies that are required and delivered in today's schools and classrooms? The current narrowing of the curriculum and a disjointed scope and sequence leads itself to drill and practice with nothing more than rote memorization. This may be the most defining and somber issue regarding the failure of communication systems in our classrooms and schools. Applying the kinderculture concept, it is apparent that many children experience their first learning with *Sesame Street* or some computer game with a fast-paced, multistimuli, and multilearning-style presentation. Is it no wonder why so many children are disinterested and disenchanted in schools, where regime and rote instruction rules? Certainly this affects motivation but we believe it also points to communication issues and to the "different languages" that are being spoken, written, and demonstrated in classrooms and homes across our country.

Perhaps one of the most overlooked aspects of communication in schools and classrooms is the fact that many teachers may view their communicative players through myopic lenses. Teachers certainly believe that they clearly communicate and receive communication from their students, parents, and colleagues, but may not realize the significance the other extended audiences have on public opinion, policy, and ultimately on the classrooms. While many of the opportunities to communicate with school boards, politicians, businesses, and media are limited in a formal sense, the communication that is unspoken sometimes has greater impact than what is spoken. It is through this lack of overt communication that we have allowed policymakers and a disjointed public to shape the current state of today's schools and classrooms, and regrettably we continue to do so.

Roadblocks to Effective Communication

So if we know what communication is and the array of communication techniques within which we engage and with whom we communicate, then what exactly is the problem? As mentioned earlier, part of the problem may be that there are numerous ways to communicate. The obvious is writing and speaking and the less obvious is nonverbal and listening. It is the less obvious ways that may be the key to reaching our students effectively. The lack of understanding the power of nonverbal communication and poor listening skills are the first roadblocks to effective communication. Let's look at nonverbal communication first.

Communication experts estimate that in face-to-face interactions only 7% of our communication is represented by the words we say, whereas 38% is represented by our sounds and how we say them, and an overwhelming 55% is represented by nonverbal actions and body language (Covey, 1998). In many classrooms where the teacher is the giver of all knowledge, it is scary to think about the impact of nonverbal communication. Just think back to the opening scenario where one novice teacher stated that she "told her students three times how to do it." She was frustrated with her students and almost angry with them for not following directions and completing the assignment as they were told. What other message was she communicating? Did the students recognize her lack of confidence, indecision or low expectations? It is important that we recognize the significance of the perceptional problems we convey to our students, parents, fellow colleagues, and administrators. The first roadblock to effective communication is misunderstanding the power of nonverbal actions and body language. Greg shares an incident between a parent and one of his assistant principals to illustrate this point.

In the course of my 20 years as principal, I've had several parents who would qualify for the decoration of "you absolutely get on my last nerve" award. One of those is very memorable and serves to illustrate the importance of nonverbal communication. During the time of this occurrence, I had an assistant principal who was extremely bright, graduated from one of the finest liberal arts institutions in the South. However, he preferred to come across with folks as just a plain ol' country boy. He often used this persona because it enabled him to "size up" situations. His intelligence and quick wit often served him well in this manner.

I was at a conference the day this particular incident occurred. The parent came to the school to question my assistant principal. She was very angry that her son had been accused of instigating a fight and was not allowed to attend the school dance, which occurred later that same day after school. Coming to school to nitpick was not a first for her; often she was at school to complain at least two or three times a week. My assistant principal met with this parent right after dismissing over 1000 middle schoolers. The parent was already sitting in his office waiting. After what had been a very difficult day, my assistant principal sat down with an umph, leaned back in his chair, placed his arms behind his head and said, "Now, what can I do for you today, Mrs. X?" Keep in mind that my assistant is very bright and had dealt with this same parent on many occasions. He thought he was being very compassionate in wanting to help and listen. However, the parent did not hear his words but took great offense to his body language. She interpreted his stance to mean, "You're not taking me seriously, you don't care about my son, and how dare you treat me with such disrespect!" She went ballistic. My assistant tried to reason with her but once the feathers are ruffled, it's hard to smooth them down again. He tried to assure her that it had just been a long day and he did care about her son and wanted to hear what she had to say. She left in a fury. My assistant called me on my cell phone (a rarity in those days) and interrupted my meeting to warn me that she had left the school and was on her way to the district office. My superintendent did see her and he listened. However, he must have used some of that same body language because now she was on her way to the governor, the state superintendent or to whomever would listen. She was on the warpath now! And here I am thinking I'm away for one short day and look what happens.

Eventually, I was able to get this parent to listen and calm down. She even agreed that her son was guilty of starting a fight and she understood the school rules about such incidences. She agreed not to press charges (for what, I don't know) and would leave her son at my school as long as my assistant had nothing more to do with her son. From now on, I was the only one allowed to deal with him. Suffice it to say that this one small act, leaning back in a chair with your arms nestled behind your head, was enough to cause serious miscommunication between school and home. It was not the words my assistant spoke, but rather the body language he communicated and the perceptions of the meaning behind them.

One can't help but wonder how this story would have proceeded if the assistant principal had leaned forward and established good eye contact and appeared to listen more intently. Often doing just that is all one needs to do to establish good communication skills. Nonverbal communication also includes our ability to interpret the very pronounced gestures and subtle posturing and eye movements that accompany our speech. Albert Scheflen (1972) suggests that body language serves the purpose of being an adjunct to verbal speech. Our nonverbal body language can support and endorse the spoken word or it can contradict the speaker's intentions. As parents, the authors of this book have said to our daughters when they've made an excuse for being a little late, "Of course we believe you," when in fact we did not. Our body language and tone clearly communicated that to our girls. Through body language one can communicate, "I have an idea," "don't do that," or "be careful" without uttering a single word. Greg often was a guest speaker in Geneal's elementary classroom and would laugh at how she could seemingly direct her second graders with only her eyebrows. Some body movements, such as shaking hands, taking someone's arm while crossing a busy street or opening a door, are part of the rituals society uses to maintain social order and to communicate kindness or respect. Nonverbal movements can also communicate fear, anger or resentment. Nonverbal communication plays an important role in how our messages are received and perceived by others.

Palmer, in his book *The Courage to Teach* (1998), states that if we want to support each other's inner lives, we must remember a simple truth: the human soul does not want to be fixed, it wants simply to be seen and *heard* (p. 11). Our inability to listen is the second roadblock to effective communication. Sometimes all teachers need to do to communicate with students, parents or a colleague is just listen. The primary goal of listening skills should be to help others express their real concerns, needs or wants. Students will often say, "I hate this class" when in actuality they are feeling frustrated over their inability to understand the material, or have concerns with a home situation or possibly have had an argument with a peer prior to class. Taking the time to listen and gather information serves to get to the root of problems with students. Listening also applies to one's colleagues. The following reflection from Greg will demonstrate the importance of just listening to one another.

> Over the course of my career I've had many opportunities to listen. Many times parents, teachers, and students would make their way into my office and I would listen, but not really. You know how that works, the teacher comes in and as I'm "listening" I'm shuffling papers and signing authorizations. I say I'm listening, but I'm not. My training to become an administrator was "old school." That school was simple; as the principal I'll tell you what to do and you do it, no questions asked. I am the general and you are the soldiers. This probably laid the groundwork for many of the missed opportunities I had to listen early in my career.
>
> On one particular occasion I had a veteran teacher come barging into my office (and I do mean barging) and say, "Greg, listen." Right off the bat she had violated

three of my rules. She entered without knocking, she sat down without permission, and she called me by my first name. My first response was, "What are you doing?" She said, "I'm going to tell you something and I think you really need to hear what I have to say!" I responded with, "You've barged into my office without permission and started speaking without permission and now you expect me to listen to what you have to say? Who do you think you are?" She proceeded to raise her voice (as I had mine) to get my attention. Despite my efforts to remove her from my office, she continued to give me some advice on a decision that I had informed the faculty of the previous day. This time I tried to appear not to be listening but I did hear enough to know that there was substance behind what she was saying. In fact, in retrospect she was giving me this advice because her heart was in the right place with both the students at our school and with me. Around four in the morning I sat up in bed and I think it was then that I finally heard what she was trying to tell me. It was an epiphany moment and probably a turning point in my career as a principal. As a matter of fact, if I was actually Saul on the road to Damascus, with the amount of times the light has shined in my eyes I'd probably be permanently blind by now! What did I learn from this? I came to terms with the fact that I could learn much by just listening to my teachers and to others around me. I could be a better principal by giving up some of my "old school" ways. I could learn and benefit from the experience of those who surrounded me.

The next day was Wednesday, faculty meeting day, a tradition in most schools. That day I called a faculty meeting and I sat them down and I just waited for a long time before I began. I said, "I listened to one of your colleagues yesterday and this time I really heard her. I decided that I want to know what each of you has to say and this time I'll listen." The question I posed was "Where do you see our school five years from now and what do you want the vision and mission of this school to be?" Slowly they began to open up and this time I listened, really listened.

This story serves to illustrate the fact that frequently we are rushed and too busy to simply listen to one another and we sometimes feel that what others have to say is not important. When forced to listen, we find ourselves merely listening with the intent to respond instead of listening with the intent to understand. What is listening? Actually there are five different levels of listening. They are ignoring, pretend listening, selective listening, attentive listening, and empathic listening (Covey, 1998). Ignoring is simply making no effort to listen, period. In this case you have totally tuned out the person who is trying to communicate with you. Teachers tend to get good at this when eating lunch with their students. It's been a busy, stressful morning and they just need a little adult quiet time. Ignoring lunch chatter can give teachers a much-needed break. Pretend listening is practiced when we pretend to listen to the speaker by giving outward appearances that we are indeed listening. Teachers who are busy grading papers while listening to their students describe their weekend is a good example of pretend listening. Selective listening occurs when we hear only part of the conversation that interests us. Spouses often use this strategy in an attempt to tune the other out or to give him or her more time to plan a response to a request! Paying attention and focusing on what the speaker is trying to say and comparing that to one's own experiences is the practice of attentive listening. An example is a conversation with a novice teacher where that teacher describes his or her day and this evokes memories of one's early years of teaching. Finally, the fifth level of listening is empathic listening. It occurs when we listen and respond with both the heart and the mind for the purpose of understanding the speaker's intent and feelings. Teachers should learn to listen with empathic, nonevaluative ears so that their students have a sense that their opinions and ideas are accepted in a nonjudgmental manner.

Listening is not an easy skill. Effective teachers know that one of the ways to listen carefully is to listen with senses other than hearing. Logging, either formally or informally, the behaviors, attitudes, and performances of students with regard to environmental stimuli sets the stage for what the authors of this book call "forensic listening." This can best be illustrated by the following story from Greg's experience as principal.

> How often have we made decisions in our classrooms and schools, all with good intentions, that have ended up producing negative effects in our students; and more disturbingly, how often have we held firm to those decisions regardless of their outcomes? My personal defining moment with this concept came when I met a young man named Alvin. Alvin was a typical eighth grade student. In many respects he was no different from any of my other students in that he wanted to be popular and accepted by his peers. He didn't set the woods on fire academically but he was an above average student. He came from a single-parent home and it was the father that he lived with, not the mother, as is more typical in single-parent homes. He had three siblings, all were brothers and all were older than he. Alvin had set his course on what we often term to be a hot-and-cold student. There were days when Alvin produced, worked hard, and did well and days when Alvin was angry and did nothing; we didn't know why. However, as good administrators and teachers will do, we kept enforcing the rules and regulations on him but we didn't take the time to step back and observe or watch or do what we call "forensic listening." "Forensic listening" is a multisensory approach to delving into the underlying causes of student behaviors. One of the responsibilities that I had as principal was to maintain order and structure in a solid instructional program. Undeniably that is a noble cause and I took this role seriously. However, that year I quickly found that I could only be successful in maintaining a solid instruction program when I coupled that with forensic listening.
>
> As a principal in a very rural area of the upstate of South Carolina, we had to rely heavily on buses to transport our students to school. In the late 80s and early 90s there was such a shortage of bus drivers that many times we had to run double routes. Oftentimes it seemed that the authorities that made those decisions at the district level made them with the "squeaky wheel" theory. The buses served the neighborhoods where the more affluent families lived first (because they would be the most vocal in opposition to double routes) and our drivers made sure they got those students to

school on time. The neighborhoods where the "Alvins" lived were served last. This created an issue because too many students were arriving to school late each day and it was those students that needed our assistance the most. Because of the havoc the late buses caused to the lunchroom (students wanting to eat breakfast well after service had been terminated), I decided as the principal that our school breakfast program would no longer honor anyone who arrived at school late, including late buses. After all, instructional time is a precious commodity and nothing could be more important than student learning. While on paper this seemed like a good decision for the sake of instructional time, it wasn't a good decision for students, especially those like Alvin. All too soon I was to learn why this was not good for Alvin.

As the year progressed, we began to have increasing difficulties with Alvin. There were outbursts in class, fights on the playground, fights on the school bus, and too much noncompliance with his teachers. My assistant principals had worked with him for weeks to finally recommend to me that we consider suspension as an option should Alvin continue to get into trouble. Alvin refused to comply with school rules and was causing too many distractions in the classroom. I called Alvin to my office to talk to him and tried to reason with him about the importance of school and why it was necessary for him to follow the rules. I don't think he understood or cared about the message.

The next morning I was walking the halls as I often did and heard a commotion coming from the classroom at the end of the hall. I quickly stepped into the classroom and who should I find at the root of the disturbance but Alvin. I quickly subdued and removed him. Once again, he had arrived late and gone directly to class. Within the first hour of school he had started a fight with one of his peers and was refusing to do anything the teacher asked him to do. As Alvin and I were walking down the hall to the office he yelled many things, including, "Go to hell, I hate you, I hate this place, this school sucks." This time when I sat down with Alvin in my office I took the time to look at Alvin's face and it was almost as if I was staring at a blank set of eyes. My assistants and I had just discovered that after carefully examining and searching for patterns to Alvin's behaviors, we discovered that these events always occurred early in the day and would subside shortly after lunch. So this time instead of beginning with my usual speech about why he should obey the rules in school, I began to look for the underlying causes of his behavior. I asked if his brothers were picking on him at home or if his dad was abusing him. I asked if he had anything that he thought I should know about. It quickly became evident that the longer I talked about home, the angrier Alvin got. Finally, out of frustration I just said, "Son, maybe I should just suspend you. Is that what you want?" Alvin looked at me with those sad eyes but said angrily, "Well, maybe you just should." In reaction to his callous response, I said, "Son, what is your problem?" He paused for a second and said, "I'm hungry, damn it, I'm hungry, are you happy now? There's nothing to eat at home and you've taken breakfast away from me." It was the look on his face and the words that he spoke that stabbed my heart, his message hit home, and this boy had to take a seat. The epiphany occurred! We had all seen the signs; how could we have missed them? We had failed to use forensic listening; we'd failed to log regularly when and how often the outbursts had occurred; we'd failed to investigate what had prompted the disturbances.

I took Alvin down to the teachers' lounge and bought him a couple of packs of crackers and a coke and we sat down and talked. Actually, Alvin talked and I listened. Alvin told me that his dad was working two jobs and he really did try to do all the things that a mom would have done but he was just having a hard time. Alvin finally said, "I guess you are going to suspend me now." I said, "No son, I'm not. I'm actually going to change the policy at school. From now on if students are late to school for whatever reason, we're going to feed you if you missed breakfast at home." Not wanting to appear to be an old softy, I did return to my principal self and I told Alvin my expectations for him. I said, "In return, I expect that you will do what you are here for and that is to work hard, complete your assignments, and do your best." I think for a brief moment that Alvin and I had reached a new level of understanding, one not normally experienced by middle school students and their principal. This level of communication included Alvin understanding that I had made a mistake and that finally I had listened to his concerns and that I was going to do something about it! This epiphany moment was yet another defining event in my career as a building administrator.

As it turned out, our newly adopted policy affected more students than just Alvin. My staff and I began to use "forensic listening" to search for underlying causes of all student behaviors. We began to listen to what students wanted, to find out what students needed, and we began to mesh their needs with our needs and with what we needed to accomplish in the classroom. My teachers also began to structure their classrooms this way. We began to listen to our students; what a simple but critical concept when working with young people!

Forensic listening is listening with the senses and with the heart. It is much like empathic listening in that one listens to be understood without being judged. We provide speakers with the opportunity to express their feelings, vent emotions, and reveal their innermost thoughts. We listen not only with our ears but we also try to gather evidence by reading the emotions of the sender, by observing the sender's use of nonverbal clues such as body language and facial expressions, and by listening to the tone of the speaker's voice. Teachers who get to know their students and who really listen provide them with a mechanism to examine and clarify feelings that are often confusing and frightening. In doing this we assist in breaking down the barriers that prevent them from being successful, active learners in our classrooms. It's hard to imagine that just the simple act of careful listening to students can reduce many classroom and schoolwide problems.

A third roadblock to effective communication occurs when teachers often fail to take into account that we also communicate to others with our voice or vocal intonation. Vocal intonation refers to the melodic sounds and rhythmic patterns of our voice; simply put, it is how we express our words. Has your mother ever said to you, "Don't talk to me in that tone of voice?" Distinctive features of intonation are stress (the emphasis given to words or syllables), pitch (the highness or lowness of voice), and pause (the juncture that separates words). Far too many stories come to mind when we think about how we fail to communicate in an appropriate way with the tone of our voice. Whether it is with students, fellow colleagues, administrators, spouses or our own children, we've all no doubt found ourselves wishing we could take back words as soon as they left our mouths, not because of what we said but because of how we said them. The authors of this book have worked with well over 500 people in over a dozen schools in at least three school district settings. It is most unfortunate that at every school where we worked we stumbled upon one or two faculty/staff members who misused tone while working with students. Geneal encountered once such teacher early in her career. Geneal was walking toward her classroom one early afternoon after escorting her students down the hall to music class. As she was passing the teacher's classroom she couldn't help hearing the teacher in a harsh, loud voice talking to (not with) a student. It seemed that once again, he did not have his homework and she was proceeding to interrogate him as to why he had not completed her assignment. The tone of this teacher's voice spoke volumes about the animosity she felt toward him. Although no harsh words were spoken out loud, I knew by the tone of her voice that she felt nothing but utter contempt for this young man. Her voice clearly communicated, "How dare you not do my homework!" Geneal could not hear the boy's response to the teacher's question, but her meaning was loud and clear. With a sarcastic tone and in a very determined voice she demanded that the other students in the room stop what they were doing (an important worksheet, no less) and avert their attention to this young man. "How many of you want to be like Brad when you grow up?" she asked. "He thinks it's funny that he didn't do his homework last night. Well, I don't and I'll see to it that he does not pass my class; why, he'll probably still be in the fourth grade when he is 16 years old! Don't you think that's funny?" Even though no one thought it was funny, everyone laughed. They were too afraid not to. During their laughter Geneal walked to her classroom, closed the door, sat down, and cried. How could anyone treat a child like that, especially someone who called herself a teacher?

The next roadblock to communication is most obvious; it is simply the words we use. Typically, we intend for each message to do the job it was crafted to do; however, the problem comes when the words we choose are not received as they are delivered. Teachers send thousands of messages to their students, parents, and fellow faculty members. These verbal messages can be grouped into four global categories, each of which tends to slow or completely stop existing communication. The first of these categories can best be described as *unacceptance messages.* Unacceptance communication occurs when teachers resort to ordering, commanding or directing. Teachers who often make demands such as, "I don't want to hear it, now get back to work," or "You better turn in this assignment if you expect to pass my class," are clearly communicating unacceptance. We need to be careful here, as moralizing, preaching, and giving "shoulds" and "oughts" in the classroom might present itself as, "You should leave your personal life out of my classroom." While it may be appropriate to communicate displeasure or unacceptance from time to time, we find in our work with teachers that many of the above examples are far too common and should never be accepted as appropriate. Sadly, unacceptance communication is becoming a regular part of day-to-day classroom activity, not because of a lack of interest in the personal lives of students but because of other factors. This occurrence mostly stems from frustration, a topic that will be discussed more in depth later.

Another category of verbal messages that hinder or block communication is inadequacy or faults. This is best characterized by judging, criticizing, and blaming. Examples of this could be, "You are such a lazy kid, why can't you get anything done?" or "I wouldn't expect you to do any better, your father was the same way when he was in school." Name calling, stereotyping, and labeling also fall into this category. "Why do all of you act the same?" A high school teacher might say, "Is that the best you can do? I've seen kindergarten students draw better than that." These communications are all just words, but words that can communicate far more than what they intended to say.

A third category of verbal messages we send falls into the realm of making the student feel better by denying that there is a problem. Examples of these include false praise or agreeing. "You're a smart student, just try harder, you can figure out a way to finish this assignment." Often students misunderstand our words when we agree or sympathize. False praise is readily identified by students and is more harmful than no praise at all. This includes teachers saying, "I know exactly how you feel," when students know that there is no way they can understand the student's background or circumstances. Students sometimes interpret these messages as, "You don't understand me or you just want me to go away and not bother you." Certainly teachers must have high expectations of their students, but it should be genuine and sincere, not just shallow words.

The final category of messages we verbally communicate that may hinder true communication allows us to completely avoid the problem altogether. We often do this by being sarcastic or humoring the student. "Seems like someone got up on the wrong side of the bed!" A novice teacher was asking her students what they had for supper the previous night. She was teaching a lesson on nutrition and wanted to use real-world examples for the day's lesson. When many of the students said, "I didn't have anything for supper last night" she was at a loss for words. Not knowing how to react to such responses she chose to ignore the issue and moved on to a different topic. This category of communication may actually serve to define the current state of education both in terms of the students served and the teachers who are in the classrooms.

These examples of communication between teachers and students do, in fact, reflect much of the frustration experienced by today's teachers. Teacher burnout is at an all-time high and is being attributed to many things, depending on whom you're listening to. The authors of this volume believe that the communication gap between teachers and students, and the subsequent teacher burnout, may directly relate to the teacher's frustration concerning the environment of America's schools. Teachers burn out because of the emotional and physical energy that they must expend to maintain their authority every day. This approach results in teachers who began their careers intending to be helpers, models, guides, and caring sources of encouragement transforming into directive authoritarians in order to function in many of today's schools. Individuals who choose to become teachers do not do so, because at some point they decided, "I want to be able to tell people what to do all day long and then make them do it." The gap between expectations and reality creates a pervasive, fundamental irreconcilable difference between those who succeed and those who fail as teachers in many of our classrooms today. Communication is the key to reversing this process. The words that we use should emanate from our own internal beliefs and values—a concept that is easier said than done.

The next roadblock to communication is a relatively new discovery in many parts of the country; by that we mean that only recently has it received its current notoriety nationwide. It is simply the reality of language and cultural barriers and their effect on communication in the classroom. It wasn't too many years ago that the idea of English speakers of other languages (ESOL) was dealt with in many schools simply with the statement, "You're in America, speak English." Many schools today are working proactively to address this issue of ESOL in ways that are culturally sensitive. As we continue down the current path of high-stakes testing and the impact of limited English proficiency students in the reporting of accountability in schools, we are now being forced to address this issue and its impact on a rapidly growing population of America's students in a different arena.

The concept of ESOL has expanded in the past five years with effective programs but still many are lagging far behind the growing need. The number of

Latino children in America's public schools is increasing with growing rapidity. Approximately one third of the Latino population in this country is under age 18. Latinos comprise 15% of K–12 students overall, with a population projected to increase to 25% by 2025. Although these students and their families have high aspirations, their educational attainment is consistently lower than that of other students. Latino achievement is compromised by a variety of factors, including poverty, lack of participation in preschool programs, attendance at poor-quality elementary and secondary schools, and especially their limited English proficiency (Latinos in School: Some Facts and Findings, 2001).

These factors are also present in ethnicities other than Hispanic. In parts of the country, limited-English-proficiency students may not face the same variables or find themselves in identical school settings, yet the burden of not speaking English in a totally English-speaking country exists and the degree of difficulty that single factor poses is always the same. How can you communicate if you don't even speak the same language? As mentioned earlier, most of our teachers fit a fairly narrow demographic profile and these characteristics most definitely do not include English-proficiency problems.

So what do we do to assist this growing sector of students in overcoming the culture of American schools? Schools can facilitate limited-English-proficient students' learning and increase their attachment to the school community by providing the educational services needed to ensure their educational preparedness by means of developing a fully multicultural curriculum. The presence of multiethnic staff members can increase the students' comfort level through an innate understanding of their values and backgrounds. Schools can accommodate these students' inclination toward cooperative learning and encourage them to create study groups to enhance knowledge and combat feelings of isolation. Schools can thus be sharing places for revealing feelings about cultural dissonance. To help ESOL students broaden their choices, schools should evaluate them for special talents and place them in classes that prepare them for higher education and teach higher-order job skills, whatever their degree of English fluency. But ultimately, schools must ensure that students master the English language as they also acknowledge the value of their native language. This sounds like a tall order but is necessary to preserve a culture and its language while opening the door to the opportunities that exist for all students in an ideal world. Looking away or other examples of "head in the sand" tactics will only exacerbate the real issues that exist in today's schools. We must find ways to create and fund these programs if we are to succeed in the mission of schooling, which should be to afford equal access and expectations to all students.

In addition to language barriers, which are obvious, other barriers exist with regard to effective communication. One of the most formidable of these is that of culture. While many times cultural and language barriers coexist there are other times that same-language students are disadvantaged by the barriers of culture. This presents itself in many ways, but predominating this category is the culture of poverty, the final roadblock to communication.

One way the barrier of poverty presents itself is through the value of education. We think that it is fair to say that the level of education has a direct correlation to poverty. In other words, the more education that an individual possesses, the less likely he or she is to find himself or herself in poverty. Yet those who do find themselves in this situation often do not see education as a viable and attainable way out. This concept plays itself out in schools every day. Why is there a failure to recognize these obvious issues that affect a growing number of our students? For a long time we have known that at-risk students are likely to have parents that have had unpleasant experiences with school when they were students, yet by placing increased pressure for them to perform on tests, we are ignoring the time-consuming activity of engagement of students and the reengagement of disenfranchised parents in favor of rote instruction, hoping to inundate the student with unconnected facts and produce a new member of the "test performance club."

For education to truly accomplish the noble task of producing a generation of successful, productive lifelong learners, we must rethink the current movement that is appearing all too frequently in America's schools. There are ways to accomplish the reengagement of disenfranchised parents and students. First, schools must take the time necessary to communicate with both parents and students. Second, they should seek to understand the extended environment of their students. Simply inviting parents to school, as partners in their child's education, is no more effective than inviting students to "learn" without regard to their learning styles or motivation. Teachers must use the knowledge of their students to prescribe and engineer opportunities for parents or significant others to become involved.

A second barrier to consider, which goes along with the issue of poverty, is that of the language of poverty. In her book *A Framework for Understanding Poverty*, Dr. Ruby Payne (2001) discusses the impact of language issues as they present themselves and how they affect school success and student achievement. She uses the exploration of the different registers of language as a basis for this concept. The language of work or school operates in the formal register. This language is characterized by complete sentences and a selective word choice.

Most of us who teach don't have to think hard to find examples of students who don't speak in this register. The language of register of choice for them is the casual register, which is characterized by a vocabulary of 400 to 800 words with the word choice being general and nonspecific. In this register sentences tend to be incomplete with language clarity dependent on nonverbal clues or assists. What do these simple facts have to do with schools, schooling, and especially students who find themselves in situations of poverty?

Montano-Harmon (1991) found that the majority of poor students do not have access to the formal register of language at home. As teachers it is important for us to note that this translates in the school setting as students who cannot use the formal register. While all students use the casual register as their predominant language of choice, students who have access to formal registers can at least function in this language pattern. This is further complicated by the fact that most state tests, as well as standardized tests such as the Scholastic Aptitude Test (SAT) and American Collegiate Test (ACT), are written in formal register. Remember earlier in this book, the authors noted that the narrowing of the demographics with regard to teachers as predominantly a product of the middle class existed while the expansion of the demographics regarding students was also occurring. Many of these teachers don't realize the inability of students from poverty to change their normal casual register and function in the formal register. One can readily see the problem that this issue of formal register can present in today's schools and classrooms. The lack of vocabulary or knowledge of sentence structure and syntax prohibits students from using formal register. Teachers and students are unable to communicate with one another! It's almost as though they are speaking different languages. This is best observed by watching students in casual conversations. Much of their language comes from the use of nonverbal clues. The problem also presents itself in student writing. A writing assignment may seem an impossible task to a student who lacks exposure to the formal register. The assignment has little meaning, both for the student attempting to complete the task and for the teacher trying to read the student's finished product.

The next issue that affects the language patterns of those who find themselves in poverty is what Dr. Payne describes as class patterns of discourse (2001). By this she is referring to how information is organized. For example, in the formal register of English, it is common to get straight to the point in a conversation or discussion. However, in the casual register used most often by students of poverty, it is more common to beat around the bush. Can you begin to see the difficulties that the incongruence between these two language patterns can cause in the classroom? Further, you can begin to see the implications for communication not only with students who fall into this grouping, but also with their parents. As educators operating in the formal register of language, we tend to get straight to the point with parents, which is a foreign concept for some parents, who may even view this approach as rude or uncaring. As educators we must use what we know about language and communication to reach all of our students and their parents. This is especially true regarding those students who come to our classrooms each day who are unlike us. The movement of a student from a casual register to a formal register cannot occur overnight, and certainly not without direct instruction. This best occurs when a significant relationship exists between all the parties involved. For example, would one learn sign language if there was no significant relationship that required it (Payne, 2001)? We again must return to the fundamental levels that drive success in school—relationships and motivation. If we can find ways to increase positive relationships, provide meaningful instruction and better understand our students, including their diverse backgrounds and cultures, then we will succeed. Is this a tall order? You bet! Is the alternative devastating? Absolutely! The decision is ours.

Communication Within the Classroom and Between Classroom and Home

Probably the most common type of communication that teachers recognize is that of communication within the classroom and with student homes; that is, the parent or guardian. Not only is it the most obvious line of communication in our schools, it is also the most important in terms of its effectiveness in relation to student learning. So much information flows through these sources of home and school communication and much of the perception of a teacher, the school, and the system is based on this communication lifeline.

First, let's look at communication within the classroom. The authors of this book believe that regardless of grade level there are common key components in successful classroom communication strategies. Probably the most important of these are clarity and understanding. The most eloquent language is worthless if it is not understood. (Remember the previous section on "Roadblocks to Effective Communication.") Effective teachers check for understanding and have systems in place for clarification that revolve around the structure and organization of the classroom. In their classrooms communication and questioning is encouraged. It is also valued and respected. Students have ownership in their instructional choices and a feeling of democracy permeates their environment. These choices and established routines are predictable, evaluated for continued necessity, and their continued inclusion in the classroom. They are often revisited by all stakeholders. In successful classrooms all members share in the decision-making process.

Once this environment exists, the communication flows with more trust and ownership. In successful classrooms, information will flow on a predictable basis with teachers using assessment for clarity and understanding. It is the environment, not the type of communication used, that marks a master teacher. It was stated previously in this volume that relationships are the foundational key to success. This is especially true with regard to effective communication.

The next and equally important arena for communication is between the school/classroom and the home. Positive and frequent communication between schools and homes improves teacher-parent relationships. It is without question that if parents and teachers are working together for the benefit of the child, positive results will occur for the student in the form of better grades, improved self-esteem, positive feelings toward school and learning, and overall satisfaction with the schooling process. The more teachers seek parents' input and involve them in decision-making activities, the more likely the parents are to take an active role in their children's education.

This is the type of communication that can make or break a teacher in many ways. In order to make it work, there should first be a communication regimen or routine established; that is, parents would be given certain information from teachers at the same approximate time of the week, month or academic term. A major challenge for teachers today is finding avenues to communicate with parents on a regular basis. This can be in the form of letters, e-mails, weekly newsletters, postcards, phone calls, parent meetings, web pages, individual conferences, home visits, graded work sent home, and open houses. Effective teachers do not just use only one of these avenues of communication, but rather they use multiple ones regularly. It is this system that not only informs the parent, but also establishes in the parent a level of trust and confidence in the teacher. This type of information flow occurs with greater frequency in the lower grades but is just as important in middle and high school. Middle and high school teachers will argue (or use the excuse) that they are "teaching" responsibility and the students should tell their parents when they are not doing well in school. It is often true that students should but many don't for various reasons. One reason could be that their parents don't want to know. Another is that it is possible that students fear what will happen to them if their parents find out about their low grades. We believe that when teachers wait until the end of an academic term to communicate a student's progress or lack thereof, they are probably committing educational malpractice. Open, honest lines of communication are critical to each child's success in the classroom.

There are times when teachers need to communicate with the home in a way that deviates from the above-mentioned form of reporting, keeping the channels open for partnerships between home and school. These special communications are driven by situations that occur within the classroom and are informational, from the sense of something that needs to be reported to the parents and they may solicit parent/guardian support. One example is an occasion when teachers need to give necessary information updates to parents. These are relatively simple in nature and usually do not cause difficulties for teachers. However, occasionally incidences of a negative nature occur in the classroom which must be reported to parents. These situations solicit support of the teacher from parents regarding their children's lack of compliance or performance in the classroom. For example, this could be something as simple as a student not turning in his or her homework or it could be of a more serious nature such as cheating on a test.

The drawbacks of regular communication with parents can include, but are not limited, to the realization that some parents are not concerned about events and programs in the schools; some parents are not capable of helping their children with assignments or projects; teachers who do not have enough time to initiate contact; teachers who do not see the importance of working with parents; parents who had bad experiences at school themselves and thus have predetermined negative opinions about school; and a general lack of the trust necessary for building the relationship between school and home. The authors of this volume believe that using regular communication channels to inform parents of student's successes establishes a level of teacher credibility with regard to teacher-parent relationships. In fact, a teacher's first contact with a parent should be positive in nature. Effective teachers will call parents with good news about everything from performance in academic areas, to behavior, to enthusiasm during an activity. By establishing a positive relationship with parents, teachers may be able to take away the most famous parent excuse, "You really don't like my child, do you?" Most of the communication of this genre lends itself to what can be termed "thinking three moves down the chessboard." This means that most situational communications in reality revolve around negative issues and that the teacher needs to draw on knowledge of the student, parent, and other information to plot the course that moves in the direction of what is in the best interest of the student, always moving toward achievement, and the use of all occurrences as learning experiences. Effective teachers are able to communicate honestly with their parents and they don't stop at sharing the hard facts. By using the knowledge of the student's needs and background, they are able to propose and discuss potential solutions with the parents. This both belies the anxiety of the parent and strengthens the role of the teacher as the professional educator. Teachers who are effective in the classroom regularly use a variety of communication techniques to establish this "long-distance" relationship with parents so that when these difficult, problematic situations occur, the real issue can be addressed without first having to peel away layers of excuses and denial. Parents are much like students in that they don't trust the teacher until they know he or she cares. It is hard to be successful without support from the home.

Communication Beyond Our Control

To this point, we have discussed communication that emanates primarily from the teacher or school. However, there is a whole category of information exchange and evaluation that is well beyond our control. All of our experience tells us that when we control something, even to a small degree, then we have a better chance to guide the situation to an outcome that is at least within the confines and constraints of our perceived vision. From where does this "communication beyond our control" emanate? First and foremost, it comes from the media messages that bombard America 24 hours a day. Across this country, from small communities to large metropolitan areas, the media support of education as part of an infrastructure to the success of this country has met with mixed reviews. In some situations it has been hailed as the savior of business development and economic growth and in others maligned as the cause of all the ills we experience as a country. This may be the single most dangerous component of today's "troubled times." The use of sound bites, half truths, and available data being used to support antieducation positions and campaigns is often beyond our control as professional educators. The media uses information for its own purposes; a fact that is in conflict with the true intent for which it was designed to confirm. A case in point is how the media uses reported results of the SAT as a predictor of school effectiveness or school quality, when in fact the test was designed to measure a student's readiness for and predicted success in college. This use or misuse of information is complex and we will not try to cover it in detail here; it is the sort of thing that teachers encounter every day. Figures can lie and liars can figure!

The reality is that many public schools produce phenomenal results despite seemingly insurmountable odds, yet these success stories are rarely, if ever, mentioned by the press or other media outlets. Only on extremely slow news days do education stories of this nature appear, and even then such stories often end up being turned into negative stories about funding, test scores or other issues.

So what do we do? Understanding what is happening is the key to overcoming it. We must mount a grassroots effort to counteract the current negative portrayal of education by the media. If we do not tell "our story," no one else will. We should tell our story to parents, community members, local newspapers, and local and state businesses. We should tell our story to everyone who will listen.

The other area of communication "beyond our control" is far more indiscernible and may be more difficult to deal with than that of the media. Simply put, this is the word of mouth that exists regarding our own perceived classroom performance that is transmitted in many cases by spectators who do not have the story straight. During our work with novice teachers, we talk about establishing their reputation with parents, colleagues, and community members. Many times in our careers we have seen teachers experience the negative side of this type of informal "word of mouth" communication. Usually this starts with one negative parent who finds himself or herself with a willing audience at a community event, church meeting, grocery story or other public place and proceeds to share "their concerns" with someone about a particular teacher and the problems that ensued with their child. The gossip travels through the grapevine and usually presents itself in full force at the time of class assignments and ends with a conference with the principal, where the parent explains, "I don't want my child in that teacher's class," even though that parent doesn't even know the teacher but only heard these comments casually. We can guard against this type of communication first merely by realizing that it exists. Care in relationship development and knowledge of overall communication strategies plus building one's reputation are the best defenses for "word-of-mouth" episodes. Positive communication techniques help to lessen the audience for the individual who seeks to use a teacher as a scapegoat for his or her own shortcomings or those of the student.

Although this does not occur often, it only takes once to make a negative impact on the lives of particularly young teachers. Remember, always do what is in the best interest of all students and for the most part things will take care of themselves. If we couple this with effective communication skills and an understanding of the environment, we will prevail.

Conclusion

Tomorrow's students must be able to communicate with people from diverse cultures, backgrounds, and surroundings. Their ability to create a better world in the future will depend on our willingness to celebrate our rich diversity through the kind of communication that leads to understanding, friendly social relations, and the building of cohesive teams. In pursuit of this notion, we must strive to create democratic classrooms that are supported by democratic practices. Classrooms set up in this manner provide an open forum that supports and invites opportunities to freely and openly discuss issues in the school, at home or in the world. We have noted that relationships are the most elemental component of effective schools and classrooms and communication is the delivery system and the glue that connects this foundational structure. By understanding the interaction of the two, we begin to get a clearer picture of the possibilities that lie ahead as we pursue this most noble of professions. Comprehending the types of communication, the common roadblocks, and the inter- and intraclassroom factors gives us a basis to see the power that we hold in inspiring a new generation of learners.

CHAPTER 5

Protecting Your Last Nerve

Stress Management for the Profession

The term "stress" was once only a small concern for educators, especially classroom teachers. Yet today it has become one of the most prevalent reasons why classroom teachers are leaving the profession. A recent *New York Times* editorial revealed that for every 600 students entering four-year teaching programs, 180 complete them, 72 actually become teachers, and only 40 are still teaching several years later (Gregorian, 2001). What is the cause of these declining numbers? Can an eight-to-three day job nine months a year really be that stressful? After all, how hard can it be to work with kids all day? Can the causes of stress in today's classrooms be controlled or, if not controlled, can they at least be better tolerated?

One only has to analyze the job responsibilities of the classroom teacher to see the tremendous changes in the roles of teachers over the years. Requirements for teachers as outlined in a 1915 teachers' contract spelled out the following:

You will NOT marry during the term of your contract.
You are NOT to keep company with men.
You MUST be home between the hours of 8 p.m. and 6 a.m. unless attending a school function.
You MAY NOT loiter downtown in ice cream stores.
You MAY NOT travel beyond the city limits without the permission of the chairman of the board.
You MAY NOT smoke cigarettes.
You MAY NOT dress in bright colors.
You may UNDER NO CIRCUMSTANCES dye your hair.

In other words, stay out of the ice cream parlor, don't dye your hair, and voilà, teaching is easy, no stress. However, it goes without question that the students back then were very disciplined, their parents were supportive, and the job of the teacher was valued throughout the community. Today's teachers are viewed in a much different light. They play many roles and wear many different hats, such as teacher, coach, mother, father, facilitator, counselor, disciplinarian, therapist, nurse, social worker, diagnostician, evaluator, mentor, and friend. Couple this with the reality that today teachers are held in low regard, are under constant scrutiny from parents and often administrators, and receive relatively little compensation for the work that they do and the degrees they hold. After dedicating an entire career to the teaching profession, most teachers, if not all, do not make as much money as professional football players do in a single season. Is it any wonder fewer and fewer college-age adults are consciously choosing teaching as a lifelong career choice?

Today's teachers must be better equipped to cope with the increasing student diversity present in the classroom, the disintegration of the American family, various social issues in the population, lack of funding, and the general mistrust of public education exacerbated by politicians who use it as an issue at election time and the media which thrives on the "spectacularization" of the state of the profession for economic gains. Teachers must deal with all this while also being held accountable for the teaching, learning, and student progress based on a single high-stakes test administered by the state, which determines not only the quality of the school but also the effectiveness of that single teacher in the classroom. At best, teaching has to be among the top five most stressful jobs; in the same category as firefighters, police officers, and little league umpires.

What Is Stress?

"Stress" can be defined as an interaction between individuals and any source of demand (stressor) within their environment. It is anything that exerts our bodies physically, mentally, and/or emotionally. Stress results from the perception that the demands exceed one's capacity to cope. The interpretation or appraisal of stress is considered an intermediate step in the relationship between a given stressor and the individual's response to it. Stress often has a negative connotation; yet not all stress caused by something is negative. Getting married, having a baby, receiving a promotion, and landing a first teaching job are stress inducers, but all these things are usually viewed as positive changes in one's life.

Certainly, stress is present in all of our lives every day in some form or another. No profession is immune to it. Plumbers, doctors, therapists, engineers, and businesspeople alike all experience stress in the workplace. However, education comes with its own specialized collection of stress-inducing factors. An increasing lack of support from parents and administrators, disenchantment with teaching assignments (whether it is related to content, physical classroom space, extremely challenging students or overcrowded classrooms), difficulty balancing personal and professional lives, excessive paperwork unrelated to classroom practice, and the teacher's own demands placed on himself or herself by holding unrealistic expectations are just a sampling of the many faces of stress found in today's classrooms. In most workplaces, when an employee fails at an assigned task or produces a poor product, repairs or solutions are often simple. When a mechanic breaks the oil plug on an oil pan, the solution is to replace the oil pan. If a product is not living up to the standards required by higher management, the employee goes back to the drawing board to start over. Excitement approaches as you await the launch of a new product and your success is measured in dollars and cents.

Such simple fix-its is not the case in education. Often students come to us needing many "repairs," having lived in impoverished homes or crack houses, and our hands are tied. In our society we have more success in rescuing animals from cruelty and abandonment than we do from rescuing children from abusive homes. If our students (our products) aren't achieving and need extra help and remediation, we often stick them in federally funded programs laden with data that demonstrate their ineffectiveness. Sometimes retention is the recommended solution for students who don't measure up to academic standards. What do we do in such a case? We place students back in the same setting, often with the same teacher, for a dose of the same medicine that did not work the first time. In education we continue to flog the same dead horse over and over again. Yes, we do await with excitement as our students move from grade to grade toward graduation, but if we ever truly feel that we made a difference in a child's life, it is often 10 or more years later. We also watch with agony as we are good predictors of students who will not make it; yet we have no power or authority to bring about the changes to stop this vicious cycle. Teaching, an eight a.m. to three p.m. job with summers off, stressful? You're damn right it is!

Causes of Stress in Educators

It occurs to the authors of this volume that one might not want to pursue education as a career choice after having read the above. That is definitely not our intent. We've experienced stress as recipients, observers, and as aides to others who are coping with it. Our passions and fundamental beliefs are grounded in the very essence of believing in the business of educating children of all ages. Has the role of teaching changed, or is it the purpose of schooling that has changed? School was once intended to teach a well-rounded liberal arts curriculum. The intent was to produce a citizenry that could think, create, assimilate, and synthesize information. What has happened today? Now we are forcing students into a more homogeneous curriculum, which is often void of many of the arts and literature programming that was once expected of students as a demonstration of their educated status.

These factors, with other demographic changes posed earlier, create the current state of affairs for those of us who call ourselves teachers. Is teaching easy, no; is it worth it, absolutely. Using a highly scientific research method of "recollecting and remembering," we'll share almost 50 years of combined teaching experience in coping with stress as educators by looking at the life cycle of a teacher through the stages of teacher development. The best place to begin this journey is with the following reflection from a first-year teacher.

> Would you believe that I was only eight years old when I realized that I wanted to be a teacher? Growing up, I loved to play school with my dolls and teddy bears. I hated summers. I loved getting ready for a new school year with new clothes, new notebooks, new pens and pencils.
>
> I could never understand those kids who didn't like school or wouldn't complete their homework. I would never, ever think of not doing my homework. Sometimes I would just copy it over to make it neater for the teacher. Ever since I can remember, I've always wanted to be a teacher.
>
> In college I couldn't wait to get into my major. I graduated with honors in December of 1978. I was ready for my first teaching job! I'd waited for this moment my whole life; I couldn't believe that I'm a real teacher!

Does this sound familiar? How many of you had some of those same thoughts and memories as you entered the teaching profession? At the beginning point in a teacher's career, teachers often romanticize about the profession; what their classroom will look like, the kinds of students they will encounter, the experience of having all eyes on them and ears listening as they explain the assignments of the day or read the next chapter in a book! This is what researchers call the *fantasy stage* of teacher development (Mauer & Zimmerman, 2000). How long does this stage last? For some, this stage will last just a few weeks; for others, a couple of days; for many, only the first few minutes of the first day. What happened to change our perception of this ideal classroom? It is the stress and reality of the profession. It has taken hold of its young and begun to eat away at all their dreams and visions for what teaching is in actuality. We all entered the profession due to our love of children; yet we find out very quickly that you can't love them into compliance. Teaching is a messy, dynamic activity and brings uncertainty, excitement, and possibilities to the forefront of daily living.

Let's take another look at what the same teacher had to say later in the school year.

> The first two weeks have been far more hectic than I could have ever imagined! I feel like I've been run over by a Mack truck! Is it possible to be this tired and still be alive? I came before school started and worked so hard to have everything ready before the first staff development day and you know what? I still wasn't ready. That first staff day was a killer. They kept throwing forms at me and notebooks for me to look over and memorize before the students arrived; fill out this form, pass this out to parents and keep the same procedures as last year. Hello, I wasn't here last year! And what's with all these acronyms? What is the NEA? SRE? PACT? No one told me decoding skills were a prerequisite for this position!
>
> Is being ready or having everything done even possible in this profession? Are you ever finished? My professor in my induction course says some funny things like "you can't eat an elephant in one sitting" or "it took Noah over 40 days to build the ark." I don't care about that, I want to know if I will ever get caught up.
>
> "Overwhelming" is a word that has taken on a whole new meaning for me. I never knew how much work teaching would be or just how exhausting it is to give 100% all day and still go home to grade papers and get ready for the next day. How do people do this year after year? I find myself so thankful in the middle of the day for a chance to sit down and just rest or even go to the bathroom. That's another prerequisite I didn't know you needed for this job—a big bladder!
>
> I will have to say that things are getting a little better. I am making progress each day with the routines of the day and more importantly with my students. The second word that has taken on new meaning to me is STRESS! I feel so responsible and so much pressure from all angles. My mentor keeps telling me to hang in there and it will get better. Well, I'm trying to follow her advice but some days I just wonder if it is all worth it.

Stage two of teacher development is appropriately named the *survival stage* (Mauer & Zimmerman, 2000). This is the time when beginning teachers often become inundated by situations and problems they did not anticipate, and discover that it takes an enormous amount of time and energy to plan lessons, communicate with parents, learn the routines and procedures of the school, and complete paperwork for the office. The novice teacher in the reflection above is experiencing the feeling of never being finished. Let's take one example of this dilemma—papers to grade. First we take the papers home to grade, we grade them immediately, and bring them back the next day. However, as the year progresses and there is more and more to do, we find this situation getting out of hand. We still take the papers home, but now we don't get around to grading them, so we just bring them back. We take them home, we bring them back, we take them home, and we bring them back. Eventually the pile begins to grow and overtakes a whole section of our bookshelves, maybe even the back seat of our car, or maybe even the trunk! After all, out of sight, out of mind, right?

Contrast this with the business world, where such scenarios are not the norm. For example, lawyers have secretaries to take care of many of the menial duties that teachers must perform themselves. The result is often that teachers become frustrated when asked to do a single thing more, become bitter and say, "Not me; I've had my turn, let the new teacher do it." It might be only the second week of school and you are already counting the number of days left in the school year. This is stress at its best.

Teaching ranks high on the list of jobs that are considered most stressful. Ironically, it is the caring quality that makes a teacher exemplary that can lead to much of the anxiety and stress experienced by teachers in the classroom. Stress exists not only in the mind but also in the body. In stressful situations, messages from the brain stimulate nerves and chemical reactions, which cause a rush of adrenaline, gearing up your body up for action. High blood pressure, ulcers, frequent headaches, and a loss of sleep are some of the many symptoms of excessive stress. The exodus from the teaching profession by both induction and veteran teachers can be attributed in part to too much stress in the workplace, or what has been coined "teacher burnout." In a recent presentation to a group of induction teachers, the authors of this volume presented some warning signals as signs that teachers are operating under too much stress. Although the examples we gave are often humorous in nature, they do provide some provocative insight into the uniqueness of the profession. We took a little creative license from Jeff Foxworthy (a true Southern humorist) in this endeavor. Following are the warning signals that a teacher is under too much stress.

- *You might be a teacher under too much stress if you put off making out your test for Monday until eleven p.m. on Sunday night.* Many teachers find themselves in this situation—unmotivated and frustrated. Teaching is never-ending, and there is always something to do. Once you finish one item on your list, a new one is added. Procrastination and a general lack of enthusiasm are certainly warning signals of too much stress.

- *You might be a teacher under too much stress if you're too tired to answer the door and you know it's the Publisher's Clearinghouse Prize Patrol car, or when you answer the phone after work, you are so tired that you say hell, instead of hello.* Excessive tiredness, lack of energy, and fatigue are warning signs of too much stress.

Geneal loves to garden and spends time during the summer pulling weeds, picking beans or staking tomato plants. She can work in the heat of the day, all day long, and not be as tired as working one day in an air-conditioned classroom. Mental fatigue can be more exhaustive than hard physical labor.

Other warning signals of too much stress are constant complaining, feeling bored, attributing self-power to others, and becoming easily irritated or annoyed. Understanding and recognizing stress is important; your challenges seem more manageable if you expect them and come to understand them.

Let's check in with our induction teacher to see how she is managing her stress now.

> I think the biggest thing that I have been learning these past few months is the depth and responsibility of my role as a teacher. At the first of the year I felt like I was drowning in all the responsibilities of a teacher, you know, planning lessons, running off papers, working with parents. I've gotten better at prioritizing my list and have accepted the fact that I will always have something on my list of things to do. At least I've come to terms with that and can actually plan more than just one day at a time.
>
> What I have realized, however, is the depth of my role as a professional educator. I have come to realize that my thoughts, actions, and words affect my students in more ways than I ever realized they would. The potential I have to make a difference in the lives of my students is unimaginable; at times too scary for me to even think about. I have the power to hurt or the power to heal. And as much as I hate to admit it, sometimes the first one is easier to accomplish.
>
> My greatest struggle continues to be my ability to meet the individual needs of my children. I have students who are reading two years above grade level and those who still don't know the letters of the alphabet. I have students who are neglected and come to school dirty and hungry and those who look like they stepped out of an ad for Gap kids. I had a conference with a mom yesterday. I mentioned to her that Sarah was not turning in her homework or bringing back signed papers. Her mom proceeded to yell at her and told her that she was stupid and just like her dad, she would never amount to anything. She is six years old. How could anyone, especially a mother, talk to a child like that? I couldn't help but wonder if she talks to her like that in front of me, what does she say to her when no one else is around. I tried to reassure Sarah that she was a good girl and that if we worked together to help her, that this would be a good school year. She believed her mother, I don't think she'll ever believe me.
>
> How can I do this for the rest of my life? Can my heart possibly take much more of this? I don't think I have what it takes to be a teacher after all.

Stage three of teacher development is known as the *disillusionment stage* (Mauer & Zimmerman, 2000). For most teachers it occurs well into the second semester of the school year. Open houses and parent-teacher conferences have already taken place, report cards have gone out, many stressful events have come and gone, and it is a time when teachers are not only overwhelmed but also disillusioned. This is a danger zone for novice teachers, a time when they begin to question whether or not teaching is really the right career of choice. Thoughts like, "I don't think I can do this the rest of my life" or "Why bother," coupled with the increasing lack of respect and support from the general public and media complicate this stage. This danger zone is and should be a growing concern for educators in all areas across the nation. Retaining teachers is becoming a critical issue in public education; not only is it difficult to attract young adults to enter the profession, now we must convince them to remain in the profession.

Research indicates that it takes a minimum of three to five years of full time teaching in the classroom to really feel comfortable and confident. Yet the expectations that parents, administrators, and even our own colleagues place on novice teachers are high; there are demands that they perform at the same level, yielding the same results as the seasoned teachers. In professional football, the first year is called the rookie year. Play-by-play commentators covering the game will excuse and even compliment the errors of rookie players on the field saying, "It's just his first year playing professional ball, he'll learn how to carry the ball so he won't fumble on third down and inches from the goal line." Doctors, architects, and lawyers all have internship years. Why not teachers? From the minute novice teachers step into their first classroom they are expected to perform like all other teachers. Are these expectations based on an uninformed public or the fact that in the current structure of schooling, there just isn't room for any deviation from this level of teacher preparedness? For whatever reason, these expectations exist and those teachers who survive must meet the challenges by adapting to the "new norms" established by many of the legislative mandates within the states of the latest federal initiative called "No Child Left Behind." Although no good teacher would ever intentionally plan to leave any child behind in terms of achievement or accomplishments, this latest example of standardized teaching, learning, and results creates a new stress-filled environment. Is it any wonder that teachers are exiting from the profession in increasing numbers? With this in mind, it is incumbent on the profession to plan systematic tactical maneuvers to develop strategies on how to best survive and thrive regardless of the stress and demands of the profession.

Proactive Strategies to Lessen Stress

The old adage "an ounce of prevention is worth a pound of cure" is certainly applicable to surviving stress in education. We believe that much of what we can do to endure and survive stress in the classroom falls into two main categories—strategies that are proactive and strategies that are reactive.

Proactive steps to stress management are dealt with throughout this book. Understanding the importance of establishing, maintaining, and nurturing positive relationships in the classroom is critical to a healthy classroom environment and also to the stress quotient of the teacher. A feeling of community which has been established between and among learners allows teaching and learning to occur. Planning relevant, meaningful lessons based on student interests and learning styles creates a win-win situation that gives students voice and power to manage the environment and arrange procedures and routines. All of these proactive steps to stress management require that the teacher enter into them by design. They don't just happen by accident. More times than not, they begin with a purposeful and reflective assessment of the teacher's own core values and beliefs as well. That is, if you don't believe that these things are important, then in fact, when you try and implement them the result is more stress, not less.

Finally, it is important to take care of yourself or as Stephen Covey (1998) proclaims in his book *Seven Habits of Highly Effective People*, "sharpen the saw." By this we mean that indeed if the saw is not sharp, it will not cut; in the same way that a teacher who is not rejuvenated doesn't teach as effectively. In order to maintain mental health and sanity, teachers must schedule time for themselves and for their families, friends, and significant others. If you're not at your best, then there is nothing left to give to your students. Failure to take care of oneself is all too common among educators. As a group, teachers are characterized by the authors as compliant people pleasers. By this we mean teachers tend to take on far too much outside of the classroom. They work with church or civic groups, sponsor activities or coordinate events. While these endeavors are desired and noble, when they become stressors they contribute to a larger problem. When this occurs, we must learn to say no and focus on our profession as well as our own health and well-being.

Reactive Strategies to Deal with Stress

Reactive strategies to deal with stress are probably more noticeable to teachers than are proactive strategies. Perhaps this is due to a stronger connection to the stress itself. For whatever reason, there are some fairly common sensical things that we can do. One reactive strategy to stress management is acknowledging and taking advantage of the importance of networking with colleagues. Talking and sharing with other teachers and staff members can help you combat teacher burnout. Teachers often experience a feeling of isolation in the classroom. Just as it is important to take time to establish relationships with your students, it is also important to develop a support network with your colleagues. A good example of the notion of isolation in the classroom is the reality that there are alternate methods of doing things. Madeline Hunter (1995), renowned educator, has estimated that teachers often make over 4,000 decisions in one day! Can you imagine that? The exasperating facet of this is that we never know if the decisions we make will be the best ones until after we make them. Take this scenario—a student is misbehaving in the back of the classroom. He is talking under his breath in reaction to almost every word you say and he is not completing any of his seatwork. How do you react? You could ignore him, walk to the back of the room and stand near him, ask him to see you after class, give him a demerit, send him to the office or send him out in the hall. If you had the luxury of time, you could run through the list in your head and evaluate each one as to its effectiveness. If you've ever spent one minute in a classroom you know that this is not possible. We can reflect on whether or not we handled the situation correctly in the aftermath, but not during the scenario. We find ourselves always looking for the *one* best answer, and that is just *not* possible when dealing with children. Your colleagues can be a huge support for you when faced with challenges such as these; take advantage of the support mechanism that is natural in healthy school cultures and environments. Teachers don't need to work harder in this area; they just need to work smarter.

Another reactive stress strategy is simply to constantly review the classroom environment, the participants, and their interactions. After all, much of the stress emanates from those factors. Look deeply at the causes of your stress in the classroom. Use forensic analysis to identify causes of stress and then develop a plan based on the facts, rather than the feelings, associated with that stress. Reflect deeply, routinely, and honestly about your teaching. It is through reflection that we learn most about how we are doing.

Next, unfortunately in today's troubled times, we must learn to react and cope with a disintegrating trust in American education and an overall devaluation of the teaching profession. How many of you have been back to your high school reunion? You see friends from the past. After they have judged you on how much hair you've lost or how much weight you've gained, they then ask what you are doing. Your response is "I'm teaching." What do they say? Either, "You're still teaching?" or "Why?" It's almost like you should apologize for still being just a teacher. If you've been in this profession long enough we guarantee that you've said more than once, "Oh, I'm just a teacher." However, you should never forget why you entered this profession. The last chapter of this text focuses on the power of the profession. That power is a central and common thread woven into the fabric of effective teachers' classrooms across the nation. Yet it is demeaning to one's self-esteem to be put in this situation and thus has a very deleterious effect on the stress of the educator. We all want to be valued and when we feel that we are not, overall stress increases.

Finally, when all else fails, laugh. Humor is important to surviving the strains and demands of the daily routines. The authors of this text feel strongly about the energy generated from humor. Suffice it to say that the old adage, "You can laugh or you can cry," is very true. We advise laughter; it has a more positive effect on your overall health as well as creating environmental conditions that will draw people to you instead of repel them.

The fourth stage of teacher development is called the *rejuvenation stage* (Mauer & Zimmerman, 2000). This stage generally occurs around the winter holidays. It comes when teachers get their second wind and are better equipped to face the day-to-day demands of teaching. Let's check on a first-year teacher we've quoted before.

> I can't believe that I'm more than halfway through my first year of teaching. I am filled with so many emotions. Part of me is so proud of the teacher I am becoming and part of me questions whether or not anything I'm doing is even right or good enough. I'm starting to get worried about the emphasis my school is placing on the *test*. Are my students learning anything? I think I'm teaching my students something. I think they will do well, but my colleagues tell me that even the smartest students fall apart on test day. Is that fair? How can I be judged on my teaching skills when I have no control over so many variables in testing? This scares me.
>
> As I look back on the school year, sometimes the only thing that kept me going was the fact that I knew my students needed me. Growing up, I always felt like I was never quite as good as my friends or even my siblings. Teaching has given me confidence. It's made me realize that although I was not a straight A student, the captain of the basketball team or whatever, I am not a failure. Teaching has taught me that there are many things that I can do and do well. I can say with great pride that I know my students know that I love them and that throughout the year I provided them with encouragement and guidance. This is why I wanted to become a teacher in the first place.
>
> When I look at the beginning of the school year I didn't see myself making it this far. It's really funny now some of the things I was so upset about in the beginning of the year. I'm better able to focus on the real reason I teach. As crazy as it sounds, I'm actually looking forward to starting my second year of teaching. I can take all that I've learned this year and make year two even better.

Is teaching stressful? Damn right it is. Is teaching worth it? Absolutely! When we were growing up we learned that nothing is ever really easy. If it's worth doing at all, then it's worth doing right. Successful teachers need the education of a president, the executive ability of a financier, the humility of a deacon, the adaptability of a chameleon, the hope of an optimist, the courage of a hero, the wisdom of a serpent, the gentleness of a dove, the patience of Job, the grace of God, and the persistence of the devil. No other profession is as critical to the realization of the American dream as that of a teacher.

Here is one last reflection by the first-year teacher written at the end of the school year.

I've been asked to write one last reflection as my first year of teaching comes to an end; not such an easy task to do, you know. I have to tell you that when I first started writing these reflections at the beginning of the year, I hated them. I just didn't see their purpose. Going back and reading them before writing this last reflection has really been a hoot. Much has happened in the short span of one year.

Let me see, what did I learn as a first-year teacher? I learned that the first day of school is more intimidating for the teacher than it is for the student. I learned that it is normal to still be reviewing procedures and routines the last week of school. I've learned to love payday! I learned that it is a daily challenge to try to teach to each student's interests and abilities. I learned that I should have respected my teachers more. I learned that all children need a hug and a kind word. I learned the importance of becoming a reflective practitioner. I learned that knowing a child's heart is the most important thing I can do as a teacher.

Just last week I learned what had to be the most surprising lesson of all. All year long I have struggled with this one parent, who also happens to be a colleague of mine. Trust me, those kinds of parents can either be the very best or the very worst. This one proved to be the latter. From the very first note that I sent home this year to the last one just a few days ago, I have always felt like I was on the judgment stand. Nothing I ever did was good enough for her son. I always felt like she talked about me to her team members, criticized my methods of managing the classroom, and constantly questioned grades and assignments. And then the unimaginable occurred. Today I received a note from her thanking me for caring so much about her son. She admitted that she had been too quick to judge me and said that she had learned much from me about teaching. I had inspired her and refueled her energy and love for teaching. Tears rolled down my face as I read those words. I never even thought she acknowledged that I was a real teacher!

My mentor once told me that teaching was like blowing dandelion seeds in the wind. She said the deeds of our hands are sprinkled and scattered throughout the land, escorted by the winds of our spirit. She said that our influence on a child's life doesn't stop when they leave our classroom; it just multiplies and blows in the wind! I often hear veteran teachers talk about letters such as the one I received today. They tell me how much something so small will come to mean to you. It encourages me to know that I too have now been on the receiving end of those moments. I know now that I was given the gift of teaching to share with others. Choosing to give it back has blessed me in return. Despite all the trials, challenges, and heartaches of this first year, I look forward to returning next year and many more years to come. Despite all that comes with the job of teaching, I know I have the greatest job in the world. I teach. I touch lives!

The fifth and final stage of teacher development is called the *mature stage* (Mauer & Zimmerman, 2000). Although the authors of this volume have dealt with stress by examining the life of a new teacher, *all* teachers may progress through all these stages or some of them each year. The authors are blessed with two lovely daughters, born 16 months apart. Both are bright, hard working, goal oriented, and delightful to be around. Greg was asked on numerous occasions when the girls were young if we were going to "try again" (some backwoods

Southern notion about the desire to have a son to carry on the family name). His response was always the same: He was very proud of his daughters and was perfectly content to be a father of just two girls. In light of this, we worked hard to raise our daughters to be more than just girls. We wanted them to see beyond gender issues as they grew into adulthood. We raised them to have high moral standards, be independent thinkers and doers, and taught them not to make excuses for the mistakes they made or when things did not go their way. We feel strongly that you are either part of the problem or part of the solution, so we taught our daughters to strive to look for solutions when dealing with adversity. Our oldest daughter is facing such adversity now; she is studying to be a teacher. Many fellow educators have questioned us as to why we did not discourage her from going into teaching. Some of her college friends laugh at her chosen major. Greg is a personnel director for a medium-sized school district, in which capacity he interviews hundreds of preservice teachers each year. Invariably he always asks the teacher candidate what his or her parents do for a living. If he finds that their parents are in education and they still freely choose to go into education knowing the hazards of the profession, he almost always hires them. Amidst all the stress and challenges of teaching, we still believe in its foundation, its premise, its philosophy, and purpose for America. Yeats said, "Teaching is not the filling of the pail, but the lighting of a fire." It is our hope that as you learn to cope with the stress, challenges, and demands of the profession that you never lose sight of your real purpose in educating our children by lighting fires and filling pails.

CHAPTER 6

But I've Already Graduated!

The Importance of Continued Professional Development

"The road to hell is paved with good intentions." This well-known proverb certainly has numerous implications for many aspects of life. It could refer to a child attempting to help clear the dinner dishes only to have them end up on the kitchen floor, or it could conjure memories of your spouse volunteering to go to the bank to transfer funds to your checking account only to remember those efforts after the bank has closed and the car payment is already in the mail! Both serve as examples of good intentions; both have results that are not exactly favorable. We submit that this proverb can especially be true with regard to teaching and professional development. Good intentions alone will not produce students who are motivated, behave or even begin to understand much less reach their potential. We have said before that you can't love children into compliance or achievement.

The professional development of teachers comes with good intentions, too. District office staffs brag about well-thought-out staff development—often a one-size-fits-all effort—designed to meet the needs of all teachers in grades K–12. However, many teachers think of it only as a necessary evil and something that must be tolerated to maintain their jobs or to get a day off later in the school year. Teachers often complain that many staff development programs have "nothing to do with them" and that they have more important things to do, especially on days when students do not report to school. No matter how impressive the plans appear on paper, many teachers just do not see the value or importance of professional development.

This mind-set is one that defiantly needs to change. How many of us would want to go to a doctor who does not keep up with the latest research, medical breakthroughs, and technology? Imagine going to a doctor who still practiced the same way that doctors did over 100 years ago! Thankfully, teachers have changed over the last 100 years, but many still teach the same way they were taught, which is in direct conflict with the current research on how students learn. As teachers, we are sometimes our own worst enemy. We complain when the general public does not treat us as professionals, but we also complain when we are required to keep our teaching credentials current, participate in staff development or attend a workshop. The authors of this book don't want to imply that all teachers behave this way. Through our many years of experience we have had the opportunity to work with numerous outstanding professionals in the field of education. We believe that educators must embrace and tackle the challenge to exemplify, embody, and accept the role of teachers as scholars and leaders in our schools. This simple concept will prove to be the important catalyst in righting the sinking ship in which educators now find themselves. This "sinking" is due to many things—the current state of high-stakes testing, narrowly focused accountability, standards-driven curriculum, and the general lack of enthusiasm and public support that exist for our schools today. Professional development, which is designed to create, nurture, and train highly qualified professionals, is paramount as a strategy to help solve the problems and challenges that we face in our public schools. Teachers who have confidence in their abilities, thirst for knowledge, and embrace educational theories not only better themselves, but they also positively affect the students in their classrooms. Professional development helps us to stretch our minds, be current with best practices, and to see "outside the box" for possible solutions. In her book *Notebooks of the Mind: Explorations of Thinking* (1997), Vera John-Steiner states that each time a person completes a novel, a research project or a composition, he or she discovers new, unresolved issues that have to be addressed. In creative work, a single product is just a temporary resting place in the continuing and demanding process (p. 85). The authors of this book like to think of teaching in the same manner. Teaching is indeed creative work and it is never constant, but rather always changing. Once we think we have something figured out, it changes! Professional development keeps us fresh and steers us toward scholarly thinking and continued self-improvement.

Recertification Versus Professional Development

The challenges and rewards of the teaching profession have never been greater. The range of information that students need to know far exceeds that of previous decades, especially in light of increasing academic expectations for all students in virtually every state and community in the nation. Each year, more information is available to educators regarding how students learn, how the brain works, the effects of the environment on student learning, and so forth. Yet many teachers don't see the connection between keeping abreast of current research and professional development and a positive change in student achievement. They still view professional development as an obligatory activity that occurs periodically during the school year that has no impact on either their behavior or on the classroom. Most states have requirements in place that force teachers to participate in activities designed to renew their teaching license. These can include college courses, workshops or attendance at professional conferences for an identified number of hours. However, do these activities actually qualify as professional growth and development? The authors of this book believe that these activities constitute externally prescribed solutions using available resources for problems within the school and/or district as opposed to a more holistic view of the professional development of an individual teacher. These externally prescribed solutions and subsequent activities are deficit-based approaches instead of competency-based approaches, which takes into consideration each teacher's knowledge, skills, and experiences. This is true regarding the novice teacher up to the advanced practitioner. This shift away from dependency on external sources for professional development to the teacher's involvement in professional development is a growing trend in many schools and one that is necessary for true professional growth and development to occur.

A change of this nature requires a vast shift in the current professional development culture. The very nature of staff development must shift from isolated learning and the occasional workshop to a more focused ongoing organizational plan built on collaborative reflection, action research, and inquiry. No longer will the skill-training model of professional development be enough. The initial training must be followed up with ongoing activities/workshops that will serve to embed these new practices into the school culture of learning within a growing professional community. The authors of this volume find it ironic that much of what is practiced incorrectly in our classrooms is also noticeable in professional development practices, a one-size-fits-all, and cover, cover, cover curriculum.

Typically, many current professional development programs do not allow for time to be built into the school day where teachers can participate in collaborative activities such as research, understanding and practicing new skills, and writing curriculum or discussion groups focused on professional articles and books. Further, in this state of accountability, it is often frowned upon for teachers to be engaged in activities other than direct student contact during school hours. Where state legislatures and school budgets have not cut out funds for teachers to attend conferences, many teachers feel guilty about attending and being away from their classrooms for professional development activities. This is perhaps due to pressure from parents, students, and administrators, or it could be due to the overall current professional culture of the school.

Given these considerations, what makes effective professional development different from that of staff development or recertification activities? Can activities even be created that can be presented to the group yet, meet the needs of individual teachers? If professional development is a potential key to improving schools, then what components exist in those that are effective? We have participated, planned, and presented in numerous professional development activities. Through all these experiences we have developed the following list of what we believe are essential components in a true professional development program.

- The program is ongoing.

- It includes training, practice, and feedback; opportunities for individual reflection and group inquiry related to practice; and coaching or other follow-up procedures.

- True professional development is school-based and embedded in teachers' work.

- It is collaborative, and provides opportunities for teachers to interact with peers.

- Effective professional development focuses on student learning, which should, in part, guide assessment of its effectiveness.

- It encourages and supports school-based and teacher initiatives.

- True professional development is rooted in the knowledge base for teaching and it incorporates constructivist approaches to teaching and learning.

- It recognizes teachers as professionals and adult learners, and provides adequate time and follow-up support.

- It is accessible and inclusive.

Having said that, we believe it is possible to have these types of professional development programs in many different settings and situations. The most essential element in the development of these activities is that of teacher ownership, leadership, and input. For schools to truly improve, teachers must be catalysts, by exerting their professional responsibility to the future of schools. This can only be initiated and realized through a series of steps, beginning with the teachers taking ownership, or at least participating in the prescription of their own professional development needs.

Assessing Your Professional Development Needs

If you believe teachers must emerge as leaders and guides for their own futures, then it is easy to understand the necessity of the individual nature of professional development activities. The authors discussed in chapters 1 and 2 the fallacy of a one-size-fits-all concept in establishing relationships with students and motivating them. Professional development for teachers is no different. For any professional development plan to be effective, it must be individualized. This begins with a thorough introspective assessment of the teacher's own needs. This sounds simple enough, right? However, several areas of concern present difficulties. First, the teacher's ability to actually conduct a personal assessment of professional needs must not be taken for granted. If we consider this in the context of the realities of teacher development, it is easy to see that novice teachers possess very different concerns than do veteran teachers. Their needs in the early years revolve around day-to-day coping, experiencing many firsts such as a confrontation with a student or a difficult parent, and, of course, developing survival skills. It is difficult for novice teachers to truly see their professional growth needs, much less be able to identify and act on them. In addition, there are some veteran teachers who view their professional work and classrooms with blinders on, meaning that they have a much higher opinion of themselves than what is accurate. This type of teacher does not approach his or her own performance in the classroom through a realistic lens. Greg was recently on an awards committee that was visiting a high school. While speaking with and interviewing many of the teachers on staff he asked them what plans they had to change their curriculum to meet the new state standards. In South Carolina the mandated state testing was well in place in the elementary and middle schools, but this year would be the year that high school students were given the test with the new standards. The responses he received from the teachers were both expected and indicative of the current state of teachers' views of professional development. One veteran teacher simply said, "I teach English, this won't affect me," while another added, "I'm not concerned, I teach chemistry." These responses require basically the same remedy; that is, an environment for a true self-assessment which identifies strengths and weaknesses of the individual teacher, moving them toward being more effective in the classroom. Suffice it to say, this may be a formidable obstacle to the desired outcome due to the realities of current school cultures. Effective self-assessment measures work best with professional collaboration through mentoring and peer coaching. As a profession, we do not normally operate in an environment of professional interaction outside the classroom. However, our experience leads us to believe that the most effective teachers do collaborate and seek advice and support from their peers.

Second, most teachers are uncomfortable with the concept of data-driven decision making. We are in a "feeling" profession and consequently many times make decisions that stem from feelings. While the authors of this book do acknowledge that using intuitive feelings can be effective, the decisions made from these feelings may be more compatible in the areas of building relationships and classroom community. As educators we tend to think of data with a narrow view of test scores and other readily quantifiable information. However, there are other areas of teaching that produce data. Often teachers are either untrained or unaware of these or the potential for their use in improving student achievement. These include student behavior records, assignment completion rates, student reflections, and other survey information relating to student satisfaction and student success. Effective teachers constantly use all data available to diagnose classroom performance and prepare for maximizing classroom possibilities. In order to assess their own needs, teachers must understand that data are important. Classroom teachers need to recognize and take advantage of the data that are available and use it in the development of a personal professional development plan.

Third, it is important to note that the availability of programming to meet the identified professional development needs may be somewhat limited. That is, many of the areas of greatest needs that teachers have reside in the realities of the classroom. Thus there are limited resources and programs, and often few individuals who can successfully connect programming to those needs. Many school districts plan staff/professional development with the masses (one size fits all) in mind. This is often due to funding issues, and the unavailability of resources, programs or consultants to address those needs. General staff development programs for the "general teacher" can be frustrating to teachers who are confident in their own skills and in identifying their own training needs. The establishment and development of professional relationships with colleagues in other schools and districts in order to share opportunities, as well as voicing their concerns and needs to the school and district administration, are both viable approaches to overcoming this problem. Again, the development of an individual professional growth plan may help to better guarantee availability of opportunities, viable professional development, and more importantly, results!

Finally, most current organizational structures of schools do not allow time for professional collaboration opportunities. We believe that it is this idea of professional dialogue that is at the center of true professional growth and development. By providing time for discussion, planning, and peer feedback, schools are better able to reach the deeper meaning and purpose of professional development. This concept of professional collaboration must be lobbied for and included in school structures. Professional collaboration is not only a valuable tool to improve test scores and create best practices in the classroom, it is also important in supporting and retaining new teachers through the difficult and stressful times of day-to-day teaching. As a teacher in residence at a small liberal arts college in the Southeast, Geneal works with mentor teachers as they work with the university graduates. One particular mentor, Ryan, was extremely good at establishing supportive, nurturing relationships with her induction teachers in order for them to grow into caring, competent, confident teachers. The following excerpt is a reflection told by Ryan.

> Michelle and I have started our own book club. We are reading a book she suggested and we meet to discuss a chapter at a time. The chapter we discussed last night was called, "A 'Dee Dah Day'" and it is about the pursuit of joy. Although I am the mentor I quickly realized after this reading that Michelle is my "joy mentor." What I loved about this chapter and find applies to my work is "strategic celebration"; that is celebration that involves activities that bring pleasure—gathering with people we love. This year, my group of first-year teachers has employed this philosophy. We believe strongly in celebrating our successes, our friendship, our efforts, our endurance, and our support system. We love to gather and pursue pleasure. We will go to all lengths to "protect" our Tuesday evenings and find another night if anything interferes with our weekly meeting. We share and thrive from this time together! Starting this week we decided to add another element to our dinner/meeting. We are going to do an activity together each week. We have certain things we want to share and learn from one another. For example, we want Kurt to teach us all more about photography. We are beginning an annual "game night" next week. I believe that this one practice has created the sense of community that exists between the five of us. I also believe that it is this sense of community that has made this year more productive and eased the burdens of teaching. I vividly remember my first year of teaching and how lonely I felt. I often wondered if I was ever doing anything right and if teaching was the right profession for me. I wish I had the opportunity to collaborate and work closely with a mentor teacher. I am so thankful for the five new "joy carriers" in my life. I believe that I am blessed to work with them and that I don't have to be intentional about being with them. I want to be with them. They breathe new life into me.
>
> (Ryan Hungerford, mentor teacher)

The teachers Ryan was mentoring knew she believed in them. She was a master teacher released of all teaching responsibilities, and they knew she was always there for them, whether it was to sit in on a difficult teacher-parent conference or to be an extra set of hands in the classroom as they attempted a new teaching strategy. This model of an extended teacher education program with a supported induction year provided the avenue for first-year teachers to collaborate and network with peers. The business world is a good example for how collaboration can be maximized and teamwork can occur to bring about change and product improvements. Greg remembers taking his faculty to visit a large business partner that manufactured components for antilock brake systems. Prior to the visit, he asked the teachers to describe what they would see upon arrival with only the knowledge of the end result, the product created. The responses included everything from a dark, noisy greasy environment to an image of "Bubba's garage." The first thing noted by the teachers as they toured the plant was the independent work teams and the use of problem-solving skills. Too often we, as educators, become caught up in our own world and become almost oblivious to the realities that surround us. Greg's visit resulted in more emphasis on communication, problem solving, and a greater understanding of integrated curriculum for teachers. These teachers returned and implemented the changes not to serve industry, but to better connect the classroom to the real world.

While self-assessment is a necessary component of professional development, it is still an elusive element within the ranks of teachers. We must use all available opportunities to find ways to continue to grow as professionals and should perhaps begin to look in uncommon places. Hopefully by developing this area we can simultaneously develop leadership and self-reliance in our profession.

Accountability and Professional Development

Educators see professional development as an avenue to reaching the goals of many of the standards-driven, accountability-based expectations of our schools. Although this is true, it is equally important to view these activities in and of themselves as valuable to the future of the teaching profession. In any endeavor, training is critical in achieving the objectives of the organization. Whether it is training to manage the drive-through at McDonald's, training to operate the espresso machine at the local coffee shop, or training for bank tellers, all training is critical to the success of the whole organization. Teaching is no different.

What is different is that the training must meet the objectives of the teaching field with a much broader scope. Accountability cannot drive professional development activities toward a narrow scope that focuses on quick, temporary fixes. Programs must be broad-based and present long-term solutions and must ultimately be owned by the participants. Otherwise, it is much like asking people to dig a specifically sized hole in a specific time limit and then proceed to take away their tools before they start! In other words, if professional development leads toward established goals, which leads to meeting accountability standards, then to remove control from those who are ultimately accountable is almost criminal.

Professional development activities must not become events that are simply tolerated, which is often the case when the activities are planned without teacher ownership and participatory development. We once heard a tale about a teacher who died and went to heaven. Upon arrival at the pearly gates, St. Peter met the teacher and gave her the grand tour of heaven. When they came to the section of heaven designated for teachers, she was flabbergasted. The teacher saw beautifully manicured lawns, palatial houses, and a never-ending line of servants to tend to their every need. However, the strange thing the teacher noticed on this particular day was that no other teachers were present. When she asked St. Peter where all the teachers were he replied, "Oh, they're in hell for their monthly developmental meeting, but don't worry, they'll be back tomorrow and everything will be back to normal." Professional development does not have to be like hell. In fact, it should be just the opposite. As professional educators we must use the knowledge and skills gained from professional development workshops and activities to begin to change our schools so that we regain the real purpose of schooling, which is educating our children.

If any form of professional development is designed to improve the current status of an organization, then it seems only logical that we would look to this format as a vehicle for solving the current ills that exist in our classrooms and schools. Teachers must be active players in determining their own needs. Schools and districts should plan for that eventuality. If we exist more today than at any other time at the mercy of noneducators, most of which hold political office, then we must use our collective voice to be heard with regard to what we need to be doing within our profession. We have seen, up close and personal, in our own state, the power of even a small number of voices and their impact on pending legislation. If we make legislators aware of our interest in a particular topic and approach it not just as educators but as voters, then for the most part they listen. We should try this and actively realize our impact on the future of our profession.

Further, individual professional development plans should fit into overall school strategic plans and school professional development plans should comply or at least be complimentary of district strategic plans. Without this coordinated effort, professional development can never be a viable agent, over the long term, for the improvement of schools, which means the enhanced achievement of all students.

Recently, Geneal made a site visit to a local school as part of a visiting team to determine an Awards of Excellence presentation for the South Carolina Middle School Association (SCMSA). Although she visited more than one middle school, the one that impressed her the most was Whitlock Junior High School, which is located in Spartanburg School District Seven. The school houses grades seven through nine and has embraced the middle school concept as outlined in *Turning Points 2000* (Jackson & Davis, 2000). Whitlock Junior High was applying for the Awards of Excellence from the SCMSA in the area of Curriculum and Assessment. With a new principal at the helm, full support from the district office, and a group of teachers committed to the same vision, this school was able to achieve the unimaginable. Whitlock moved from being an unsatisfactory school as determined by the state test, Palmetto Achievement Challenge Test (PACT), to an average rating in just one year. Ninety-two percent of all students at Whitlock fall into the poverty range, with 85% classified as minorities and an overwhelming majority of students qualifying for a free or reduced lunch. How did they accomplish such a feat in such a short amount of time? Almost everyone involved in this transformation says it was how the school adopted a different approach to professional development. Kenny Blackwood was appointed principal when the school was at its lowest point. He set out to change the image of his school and to prove that all students can learn, given the right opportunities. During the summer after his first year, Mr. Blackwood held a weekend retreat with his faculty. When Kenny asked his teachers to pinpoint the most critical impediment to student success, they cited parental involvement. But it wasn't the only thing they cited. According to one veteran African American teacher on staff, "Some teachers don't believe our black students can learn. They don't expect them to do well. And it's not just the white teachers I'm talking about." In light of these comments, Geneal was curious about the school's accomplishments so she asked Mr. Blackwood to share some of his ideas and comments on how the changes occurred at his school. He wrote the following.

> First of all it is important that everyone on our staff embrace teamwork and the development of high expectations. This component is the very foundation of our program of democratic governance. We believe that all information must be shared, discussed, dissected, digested, and prioritized if the desired results are to be obtained. At Whitlock, the process began with our faculty retreat. This was a family style meeting where we openly and honestly shared our concerns and problems with an emphasis on finding a workable solution to the problem—how to go about changing the image of our school and the accomplishments of our students. Our first retreat focus was on the change process in terms of improving student learning and achievement and changes in administration. The second retreat focused on student

discipline and supervision of students. The ideas generated from the faculty at each of those retreats far surpassed what would have been accomplished if only an administrative perspective had been considered.

Mr. Blackwood is very quick to point out to visitors in his school that the credit for the success of his school does not go to him. He very proudly says that it was his teachers and his staff rolling up their sleeves and working together as a team that brought about the changes that were necessary at Whitlock. Supporting teachers means giving them the very best tools—the best research-based lessons and materials coupled with the best training available. The administration at Whitlock Junior High set out to do just that. Their philosophy about professional development was that it should be research based, ongoing, and continuous, and most importantly, it must be shared by the teachers. The professional development endeavors in which Whitlock participated had to lead to improved teaching and therefore increased student achievement. The school qualified for an on-site curriculum specialist to study and assist the teachers in revising the curriculum to meet state standards. The school also qualified for teacher specialists in the areas of language arts, math, and science to train teachers in effective practices in their particular content areas.

The teachers felt that they needed more time to work with their students. No matter how hard they tried, it just seemed that there was never enough time to accomplish what they wanted to in the classroom. So, they volunteered, *with no extra pay*, to increase the school day by 25 minutes, which gave every student a 94-minute block of instruction in math and 94 minutes of language arts instruction. Then the teachers identified about 170 students who would stay for extended instruction four days a week. They even implemented a Saturday academy for similar purposes. The district was committed to a ratio of 20 to 1 to give teachers a better opportunity to work with individual students or with small groups. The heart of their professional development focused on Ruby Payne's, *A Framework for Understanding Poverty* and Samuel Casey Carter's *No Excuses,* and *Dispelling the Myth,* a publication from the Education Trust. The district provided training in the form of workshops, conferences, and college courses focusing on *Understanding by Design* (Wiggins & McTighe, 1998), Ruth Culham's *Six Traits Writing* (2003), and much more. Mini sessions were held at faculty meetings to discuss such strategies as cooperative learning, classroom management, effective questioning, and more. These were led by teachers, most of whom were on staff at Whitlock Junior High. The schedule ensured all teachers a common 40-minute planning period each day to collaborate with their peers and plan together. Margaret Peach, an on-site curriculum specialist, shared her sentiments on professional development and the changes that have occurred at Whitlock.

> Democratic governance is the process that has been implemented since the arrival of the curriculum team and administrative team two years ago. We believe that this is the cornerstone of effective and successful schools. Our process began with the faculty retreat and continues today through a variety of venues. As a result of our retreat it was revealed that there were a number of needs and concerns that demanded a resolution. This need led to the formation of three broad committees that meet on a regular basis to design solutions to our shared problems. This process has not been easy or quick, but it has been exceedingly effective. It has required a great deal of training on the responsibilities that naturally accompany any "society" that governs itself. Ownership of a set of solutions carries with it a vested interest and commitment to the success of the program.
>
> Our Saturday academy was a prime example of moving in the direction of democratic governance. Teachers were given the freedom to develop a lesson to be taught at each of the four sessions. The only two requirements that were imposed were that research-based best practices must be used and that the lesson could not be a worksheet lesson. Our teachers rose to the occasion with gusto! They created beautifully crafted lessons with activities that excited the mind and energized the body. It was "coloring outside the line" in its finest hour. Being part of this change was one of the most rewarding experiences of my teaching career. Our greatest testimony to the program was the tremendous number of students who begged to attend and the young man who said to me after the first Saturday academy, "This is my best day of school ever, I can't wait to come back." Just tell me—what could be better than that?

What an excellent example of true, effective professional development! Teachers were empowered to take an active role in the design of the curriculum. Bridget Burts, seventh-grade language arts teacher at Whitlock, said, "We were able to think of the specific needs of our students. We thought about their interests, cultural influences, and strengths and weaknesses in order to design a program that would hook them into giving up a portion of their Saturday. The students were motivated by the attention and they felt loved." The results are in the data.

Using Reflective Practice

We asked the kids to write down some of the names their friends and family call them. They wrote things like Honey, Josh for Joshua, Sweetie Pie, Tiger, and Son. I was walking past Taylor's desk and saw that he had only written down "Taylor." "Hey, Taylor," I said, prompting him, "what's a nickname your dad has for you?" He looked up at me. "My dad mostly just calls me cuss words and I can't write those.

ERRATA

Teachers Teaching Teachers

The incomplete extract on page 117 should read as follows

How can I do this? How can I walk into a room full of children day after day and look into their eyes and see their lives reflected there? Yes, there's a lot of joy, but there's also so much pain. I didn't have anything to say to Taylor. "Gee, that's too bad, Taylor, but how about if I think up a nickname for you?" (pause as Taylor just looks at me) "Oh, gosh, Taylor, but, hey, I still love you."

There is nothing I can ever say or do to make up for or change or fix what goes on at Taylor's house. I can't teach him to read enough books that he'll be able to ignore what's happening at home. I can't love him enough to make it okay that his own father doesn't.

And in the middle of staring into Taylor's eyes and feeling the weight of all that emptiness, Lilly couldn't read this word, and L. J. wanted to take a Reading Counts test, and Christopher needed to go to the bathroom, and Kelsey had a funny story to tell me…And Taylor's daddy mostly just calls him cuss words.

So I walked away from Taylor, and Lilly and I sounded out the word, Kelsey's story really was pretty funny, L. J. scored 10 out of 10 on his test, and I didn't cry. But the yucky feeling of my heart sinking to the pit of my stomach hasn't gone away yet, and I'm not sure it will.

I wrote that part about Taylor Thursday after I got home from seminar and was feeling overburdened with endless PDs [professional dimensions] that feel like they get in the way of the real people. I was pretty discouraged.

And then Carrie, Angie, Josh, Kathryn, and I [other senior education colleagues] all had dinner together and the cruel irony of the situation hit home: We walk—okay, run—away from the seminars at the end of a long day so exhausted and sick of school and teaching and learning and everything that has to do with education, but we spend several hours fixing and eating dinner, all the while talking nonstop about our day and teaching and the education system.

Teaching is nine tenths love and commitment, which means it's laughter and tears and frustration and joys all mixed up in a package. And sometimes the packages are tied with a shiny new bow and sometimes they're wrinkled and dirty, but they're all unique and beautiful and begging to be unwrapped.

(Laurie Ingram Sibley, senior education intern)

test, and Christopher needed to go to the bathroom, and Kelsey had a funny story to tell me...And Taylor's daddy mostly just calls him cuss words.

So I walked away from Taylor, and Lilly and I sounded out the word, Kelsey's story really was pretty funny, L. J. scored 10 out of 10 on his test, and I didn't cry. But the yucky feeling of my heart sinking to the pit of my stomach hasn't gone away yet, and I'm not sure it will.

I wrote that part about Taylor Thursday after I got home from seminar and was feeling overburdened with endless PDs [professional dimensions] that feel like they get in the way of the real people. I was pretty discouraged.

And then Carrie, Angie, Josh, Kathryn, and I [other senior education colleagues] all had dinner together and the cruel irony of the situation hit home: We walk—okay, run—away from the seminars at the end of a long day so exhausted and sick of school and teaching and learning and everything that has to do with education, but we spend several hours fixing and eating dinner, all the while talking nonstop about our day and teaching and the education system.

Teaching is nine tenths love and commitment, which means it's laughter and tears and frustration and joys all mixed up in a package. And sometimes the packages are tied with a shiny new bow and sometimes they're wrinkled and dirty, but they're all unique and beautiful and begging to be unwrapped.

(Laurie Ingram Sibley, senior education intern)

Are you serious, reflective writing a professional development piece? Yes, even as long ago as 1910 John Dewey said that active, persistent, and careful consideration of any belief or supposed form of knowledge in light of the grounds that support it, and the future conclusions to which it tends, constitutes reflective thought. Just like Laurie, the senior education student quoted above, Dewey viewed reflective practice as a "felt need" that usually comes in the form of open-ended questions about methods, strategies or student learning. Through reflection Laurie is learning important lessons about the real world of teaching. The authors of this volume like to view reflective thinking/writing as something that effective teachers do naturally and intuitively. In 1989, Donald Schon introduced the concept of reflective practice as a critical process in redefining one's artistry or craft in a specific discipline. Indeed, reflection is a critical function of successful teaching and learning. It has been defined as an analytical process of data gathering and sense-making through which teachers deepen their understanding of teaching and learning (Boreen, 2000).

We believe that reflection is essential for a fully lived professional life. Effective teachers reflect and look back to mull over the day's successes, and each student's progress or lack thereof, to create and devise innovative strategies to meet the individual needs of the students in their classrooms and to plan for the next day. In education, every day is a new day and no two days are exactly alike. Seasoned teachers use reflection systematically to organize their thoughts and make sense of classroom events. Teaching is an ongoing process of process of data gathering and sense-making through which teachers deepen their understanding of teaching and learning (Boreen, 2000).

We believe that reflection is essential for a fully lived professional life. Effective teachers reflect and look back to mull over the day's successes, and each student's progress or lack thereof, to create and devise innovative strategies to meet the individual needs of the students in their classrooms and to plan for the next day. In education, every day is a new day and no two days are exactly alike. Seasoned teachers use reflection systematically to organize their thoughts and make sense of classroom events. Teaching is an ongoing process of knowledge building; it is through reflection that we are able to look for opportunities to better our practice and improve our craft. Reflection enables teachers to capture and critique what is working well and what is not. Schon (1983) recommended reflective practice as a way for beginners in a discipline to recognize consonance between their own individual practices and those of successful practitioners. All classroom teachers, novice and experienced, are faced with classrooms that are full of challenges and unexpected events. Reflection on classroom practice should not only be focused on classroom catastrophes but should also examine what is going well; once those practices are identified, intentional efforts should be made to repeat those successful activities. By examining, identifying, and focusing on successful practices, teachers are continually improving their craft and growing in their efforts toward effective teaching. The ability to look back and reflect on classroom practice allows teachers the opportunity to make sense of the flood of images, feelings, and expectations that occur on a daily basis in today's classrooms.

Schon (1983) developed two categories of reflective thinking—reflection-on-action and reflection-in-action. Reflection-on-action is a systematic analysis of professional activity or performance after a task is completed. Mentor teachers who work with novice teachers will often sit down at the end of the day to discuss the day's undertakings and brainstorm how things could have been handled differently. Supervising teachers are able to do the same after observing an intern's first lesson with the class. Reflection-in-action occurs in the midst of an activity and often results in the immediate changing of classroom actions or plans. It is this type of reflection that is the most challenging for beginning teachers. Schon (1983) declares that the most important decisions made in the classroom are made during the act of teaching. For example, a teacher is working with third graders to teach the difference between similes and metaphors. When preparing for this concept the teacher thought that she had all her bases covered and that the methods she was using to teach this skill would work with her students. However, as she was looking at the faces of her students, listening to their questions, and analyzing their confusions over the planned activity, it was apparent to her that she must do something differently, for her plans simply were not working. She has several options at her disposal. She could table the discussion or activity until another day when she would have more time to research other strategies, she could change her plans in the middle of the lesson, or she could do nothing. Often new teachers will choose to do the latter since changing the direction of a lesson or activity in midstream is difficult. Knowing where to go once you decide to change direction is even more difficult.

Reflection-in-action is usually based on nonsystematic memories of events or casual observations. Interns or novice teachers will often ask seasoned teachers how they knew how to handle a difficult situation with a student or how they thought up a new plan on the spot in the middle of a dying lesson. The answer to those questions is not always easy. We usually respond with, "I don't know, I just did." Years of experience have provided us with multiple solutions to a wide range of classroom situations. Through reflection (coupled with experience, of course), teachers are able to build up their repertoire of solutions, ideas, and strategies. Also, the value of this reflection could be increased if it was based on data collection through systematic observations. When teachers apply systematic approaches to observations and data collection, they move into the realm of action researcher.

The Teacher as a Researcher

Simply mention the word "research" to most teachers and it conjures up all sorts of horrific images. When teachers think of research they see visions of moldy books, big impersonal libraries, grouchy old librarians, and hours of pointless work. They see themselves sitting and staring at a blank computer screen not knowing how to start or where to begin on the required research paper for the professor. The truth of the matter is, teachers are naturally good researchers. Effective teachers instinctively "do it" every hour of every day in the classroom. To be truly effective, a teacher must be an active participant in the classroom and an astute observer of students. It is through careful observations that they can analyze student progress, interpret test results and data, and purposely plan and execute lessons. The results of these deliberate efforts are witnessed and exemplified in their classrooms and in their students.

As lifelong learners, teachers should practice action research to improve their own effectiveness. Action research is a mechanism for teachers to improve their practice and focus on positive changes within the classroom. It is also a viable tool for professional development. Teachers who participate in action research have increased confidence, higher self-esteem, openness to research, and a liberated creative potential for seeing solutions to classroom situations that are outside the norm. The authors of this text believe that to be successful in today's classrooms, teachers must be astute observers of their students and purveyors of solutions that are outside the norm.

We have said before that teaching is both a science and an art. Action research equates with science (the theory, if you will) and practice is equal to the teacher's artistic ability to practice and carry out that theory. Action research can be a tool for teachers to reacquaint themselves with current theory. However, theory is only useful if it can be put into practice in a classroom. Adapting a theory in response to the unique characteristics of the setting or population with whom the practice is employed can result in increased utility and effectiveness. When such adaptations are conceived and implemented with the rigors of research, data collection, and analysis of the results, this can only lead to a refinement and adjustment to the underlying theory and practice. This systematic adjustment of theory to practice and practice to theory is at the core and heart of action research.

Action research can take on many forms and employ a wide range of methodologies. The key to action research that is worthwhile is not the type of methods that are used but in the questions that are researched and the degree to which they are meaningful and effective in the classroom. Questions teachers can ask include, "What can I do to motivate my students?," "How can I teach this concept in a way my students will understand?," "How can I best help students who are from challenging backgrounds?," and "How can I manage my classroom resources and work with difficult students?" Adapting a theory in response to the unique characteristics of the setting or population with whom the practice is employed can result in increased utility and effectiveness. When such adaptations are conceived and implemented with the rigors of research, data collection, and analysis, the results can lead to a refinement and adjustment to the underlying theory. This systematic adjustment of theory to practice and practice to theory can lead to optimum results in the classroom.

Teachers as Professionals

Have you ever thought about the fact that we are in the profession from which all others are born? That is, no one becomes a doctor, a lawyer or an architect without attending a K–12 school setting with a teacher who inspired and created a classroom in which inquiry, discovery, and confidence were all present. What a powerful profession we are privileged to belong to! So why is it that teachers don't behave like people in other professions? In other industries, professional development and training are a regular part of the workday, and is viewed as essential to the individual's performance and effectiveness. In virtually every state in the country, reform efforts are dramatically raising expectations for students, and consequently for teachers. In response to these reform initiatives, educators are being asked to master new skills and accept more responsibility to change their practice. To meet these new expectations, teachers need to deepen their content knowledge and learn new methods of teaching. They need more time to work with colleagues, to critically examine the new standards being proposed, and to revise curriculum. They need opportunities to develop, master, and reflect on new approaches to working with children. All of these activities fall under the general heading of "professional development."

Historically, state policymakers have paid little attention to the form, content, and quality of professional development. Such matters have been left to the discretion of local boards of education and district administrators. However, if today's teachers are to be adequately prepared to meet the new challenges they are facing, this laissez-faire approach to professional development must come to an end. The needs are too urgent and resources too scarce to simply continue or expand today's inefficient and ineffectual arrangements.

To make this shift, teachers must enhance their knowledge of subject matter and learn to use new teaching strategies. Additionally, with a hands-on, student-centered approach to teaching, which uses more time to cover less, choices must be made about what content is essential. New assessments are needed that probe students' understanding of content and examine their ability to integrate knowledge and apply it to real-life problems. Higher academic standards require far-reaching and difficult changes in the practice of teaching. An area that contributes to dissatisfaction in professional development is that of a narrowly focused program. Within the context of high-stakes testing, much of the professional development programming revolves around quick fix, new ways to force all children to respond to the same kinds of instructional approaches. The problem of teacher dissatisfaction and disinterest results from the realities of the classroom and its incongruence with the information being force-fed by the purveyors of this type of training.

Another aspect of current reform is a shift in decision-making authority from the state agency and district central office to the school building. It is this lack of ownership of the activity that creates much of the ineffectiveness with regard to many current professional development programs. Under school-based management, teachers are taking on new roles as members of school governing boards and entering into new relationships with colleagues, school administrators, and parents. These more varied and complex roles demand new skills and new knowledge. If teachers are to be adequately prepared to work effectively in the classrooms and schools envisioned by reformers, policymakers must establish a coherent and more effective approach to professional development. Teachers and policymakers must abandon long-held conventions and beliefs about continuing education for teachers and begin to understand professional development as an essential and integral part of a teacher's work.

Finally, the current public opinion of public schooling, prompted to a large degree by the politicians and the media, doesn't allow for those in the teaching profession to believe that we are truly professionals. We are lambasted as the root of many of the problems that exist in our society. Consequently, many of our ranks respond by simply putting in the time, day in and day out, much like that of an assembly line worker with no vested interest in the end product emerging at the end of the line. How sad!

So what are we to do to turn this tide of negativism toward public education and those who teach? We believe that leadership from the ranks of teachers is essential. We must seek ways to find, develop, and exert leadership into changing the current state of teaching. The authors of this book believe that the first way to do this is to take control of our own professional development. We must help to design and participate in training that will allow us to use our knowledge of the realities of the classroom to help improve instructional opportunities and thus enhance achievement for all students. Membership in professional organizations can also be a great source of substantive professional development, for it carries with it privileges, subscriptions to professional magazines, the opportunity to attend meetings where we can collaborate with peers outside of our school, and the opportunity to attend conferences where we hear information about the latest practices, innovative classroom techniques, and new books to use in our classrooms. If we believe that learning is in fact a lifelong activity, then who better to model that than America's teachers? Teachers, you just *think* you've graduated! Isn't it wonderful that we are in a profession that can't afford ever to stop learning?

CHAPTER 7

Molder of Dreams

The Power of the Profession

I was never a person content to view life as black and white, but teaching has, more than ever, taught me to appreciate the richness of the grays in between the extremes. Seeing the grays takes many forms these days. I have learned above all to see the richness in myself. I walked into my first classroom neatly divided between two extremes: the teacher version and the home version. Some compromised version won over pretty quickly, as the relationships I have developed with my students have enriched the realness of my life and obliterated the need for a façade. My students have taught me that my greatest strength is me. This, of course, can be taken at a very simple level, or much deeper. A few examples: I love rap music. I have a tendency to spill things when I get excited. I can be horrendously stubborn. I get terribly loud hiccups. To harness myself in and glaze over the imperfections, I found, is to cheat myself and to cheat my students. To be white, when my essence is black, or vice versa, is to ignore the richness of color that lies in between. Meeting my individual students on a real but appropriate level changes the way that we are learning from each other.

To lose the black and white is to lose the stereotypes, the assumptions, and the rumors that limit my students. To refuse to see a poor kid or a rich kid, labels of a bad home life or overprotective mom, is to allow each student to define his or her own hue.

Take charcoal gray, for instance. Charcoal is dark and rich, almost tremulous with strength. Alexander is charcoal gray. At first, I overlooked him, I admit, and assumed there was only blackness there. His negative attitude and utter defiance of reason were frustrating. Soon, with hope, I caught glimmers of the richness that lay below his troubled, darkened eyes. Then, little by little, he let it leak out in bear hugs and the kind of smile that changes the way a room looks. His stubborn strength became an eager strength, one that hoped to answer a question correctly or talk for a moment in the cafeteria. When he reverts to the unresponsive boy I thought I knew, I still know hope. I have seen the charcoal in him.

Some grays are so beautiful that they shimmer, almost silver. These are the ones that are easy to love, the material for songs and evening gowns. Yet even these can fail to shimmer if I fail to look at them in the best light. Kurt shimmers in his untamed enthusiasm for all things science. He collects anything that moves and fits in an aquarium. His has an ability to portray more emotion in his pursed lips and wrinkled forehead than the greatest of actors. Kurt will do back flips to be given an opportunity to touch the class pet. He will keep his hand raised to share more information than necessary to answer a simple question. When I look out at the 30 students in my first period class, I am overwhelmed by their individual learning needs. I want to go back to sleep every morning in the middle of this class, to rewind myself back under my down comforter and hit the sleep alarm one more time. Inevitably, I catch a glimpse of shimmering silver, and, as the moment passes, I breathe again and keep teaching.

Heather gray, the color of my favorite knit sweater, is mirrored in the comfort of my relationship with Katie. Katie and I fit together perfectly. She seems to realize the full responsibility of being my student as much as I understand the full potential of being her teacher. Teaching Katie is comfortably simplistic, just like curling up inside that favorite sweater after a long day. With my blond-headed, heather gray student, teaching is just like coming home.

There are other grays as well, enough individual hues to fit my many students. Each day, children enter my classroom with colors ready to be known and unrealized hues requiring my attention. Seeing my students in black and white is not honorable, for their sake. Luckily, the pure starkness of these two blends to make an incomprehensible array of color. It was in opening myself up to this potential that I found out the power of my chosen profession, the power to recognize, inspire, and shape the color of a student. Teaching, as in life, is found in the grays.

(Megan Phillips, first-year teacher)

Teaching indeed may be found in shades of gray. We have presented throughout this text the positive aspects of teaching, as well as the challenges that we currently face in education. In this chapter, we hope to frame the profession of teaching in the context of the power that we have over the future of the country in light of the impact realized each and every day upon the children with whom we interact.

Unless you are a teacher you probably do not understand the concept of teachers having power. Power is often equated with money, authority, and control. Yet power for teachers does not come in the form of having power over someone or something. It comes from the power we have to influence and make a real difference in the lives of those we encounter in our classrooms. Most teachers are familiar with the following quote from Haim Ginott (1972):

I have come to the frightening conclusion. I am the decisive element in the classroom. It is my personal approach that creates the climate. It is my daily mood that makes the weather. As a teacher I possess a tremendous power to make a child's life miserable or joyous. I can be a tool of torture or an instrument of inspiration. I can humiliate or humor, hurt or heal. In all situations it is my response that decides whether a crisis will be escalated or de-escalated, and a child humanized or de-humanized. (pp. 15–16)

Having been born and raised in the South, we know a little about the concept of "calling." We define "calling" as a divine event in which a greater power anoints an individual to a higher level of performance. One teacher puts it as follows:

From an early age, I've known I've wanted to be a teacher. No, my parents weren't teachers, nor did I have aunts or uncles in the teaching profession. What I did have and was given were wonderful teachers who inspired me and motivated me and believed in me. I've always known I'd work with children, modeling my love of learning. I've known that I would spark interest and curiosity in my students as well as provoke questions about the world around them. Although teachers may have different reasons for teaching, I believe we all share one…our love of children.

Simply put, I love children, all kinds—from the ones who have both mom and dad at home, to the ones who know how it feels to lose a parent from overdose or suicide. I love the ones who are so self-conscious it makes you cringe to think how difficult it is for them to make a presentation in front of their peers and the ones who hate coming to school because it means they'll get picked on. I love the ones who love school because they can be someone their parents never get to see, to the ones who are gifted, to the ones who have IEPs (Individual Education Plan), to the ones in trouble all the time, and to those who know when their teacher needs a hug. I love children and I want to see them all succeed and feel successful in their endeavors, both large and small.

I believe the greatest reward in teaching is working with the children. It's also learning alongside your students. I continually search within myself and push myself daily to become an effective teacher. I still work on this. I amuse myself with the concerns I had early in my career. Early on, I was concerned with whether I would have enough books to teach from, chalk to write with, crayons for my students to color with, desks for my students to sit in, and a bathroom close by to avoid a bladder infection! I was afraid of mistakes, or even to ask questions. I wanted to be a perfect teacher. I realized quickly, however, that even good teachers make mistakes and ask dozens of questions on a daily basis…and those questions continue to come. As each school day ends, and I sit exhausted at my desk thinking about the activity of the day, I smile knowing that I have given of myself unconditionally and I have tomorrow to look forward to.

(Nicky Martinez, veteran mentor teacher)

This reflection serves as a wonderful example of those teachers who are able to rise to the occasion of meeting the challenges and creating exciting classrooms where all students cannot only learn but thrive.

What makes this transformation possible that we can leave the ordinary and move into the extraordinary? Teachers who transcend this chasm are those who set the standard for all others to follow. These are the teachers we have discussed throughout this text and whose experiences will be highlighted throughout this chapter. However, to fully understand this power of the profession of teaching, the authors of this book believe we must first take a stark, realistic look at the profession in its current state. This is not to say that upon reading this, you should become disheartened with the idea of teaching. Rather, our purpose is to be open and honest and set the foundation for the remarkable work that occurs in the classrooms of effective teachers across our country.

The Realities of Teaching

If you stay in the business long enough you will hear teachers talking about quitting the profession. In fact, we'd be willing to bet that those words are uttered in every school building regularly, sometimes even on a daily basis. Walk into a teachers' lounge and you hear teachers at one end of the lunch table saying, "I really think I could make a difference at McDonald's" or "I'd rather scan at Wal-Mart than do this every day," while at the other end of the table two teachers have their heads together conferring on the prospects of starting a catering business or bookstore. Teaching certainly is not an easy profession. As the authors have stated before, at best it is one of the most stressful careers. Where else could you find the kind of pressures, expectations, and demands that we have discussed in this text for so little compensation, respect, and recognition? Let's take a minute to look at some of the frustrating aspects of teaching. We believe that this realistic look at the current state of the teaching profession must be shared in order to better understand the true power of our profession. Later we will share some suggestions of how to continue in the field in spite of these challenges.

Probably one of the most frustrating aspects of teaching is that a teacher's job is never, ever finished! This has to be one of the biggest surprises for first-year teachers, especially those who are compulsive perfectionists. One example of this dilemma deals with paperwork. Teachers have forms to complete, reports to create, and of course papers to grade, which we discussed earlier in chapter 5. But there are other examples where teachers feel like their jobs are never finished. There are bulletin boards to make, lesson plans to write, standards to cover, committees to serve on, meetings to attend, and the list goes on and on. This is not true in other professions! Lawyers have many tasks to accomplish; however, they have secretaries to take care of many of the menial duties that teachers must perform for themselves. Doctors also have secretaries to answer the telephone, make appointments, keep records, and organize the office. Ministers have church secretaries to take care of Sunday bulletins, send out monthly newsletters, and much more. Often the result of this reality for teachers is that they become frustrated at being asked to complete one more form, serve on one more committee, or do one more thing. They become bitter. Teaching has often been dubbed the only profession that "eats its" young. In most schools, little or no support is provided during the early years of teaching. Most professional occupations have an internship or training period to help reduce the stress and provide the support needed until the new inductee feels more comfortable and confident in his or her new position. A common complaint among all teachers is that they are being asked to do more with less time and no help. Is it any wonder that the exodus from the profession is ever growing—almost 30% leave after just two years of teaching?

A second frustrating reality for teachers was also discussed in chapter 5, which was the reality that teachers have alternate methods of doing things. The example given was that of a teacher not knowing exactly how to handle a discipline situation in the classroom. As educators, we find ourselves always looking for the one best answer, and that is not always possible when dealing with children. During the summers in college, Geneal was a bank teller. After two weeks of training and working with another teller right by her side, watching every move she made, Geneal was ready to man a teller window on her own. Even then she was given advice on how to specifically handle various transactions. If she was unsure how to handle a new transaction all she had to do was to refer to her "how-to" notes, or better yet, ask the head teller who happened to be working right beside her. Did you know that customers are even willing to wait so that you handle his or her transaction correctly? This is not true in schools and classrooms. There is no "head teller" to assist the teacher in the classroom and to point to the one solution on the prescribed "how-to" list that was generated during training. Also, unlike the customers in a bank, parents are not always willing to wait. Most parents, if responding honestly, would not care about the intricate relationships that occur in a classroom. Their only concern is that single relationship between their child and the teacher. Where the issue comes is when the complexities of the classroom do not run parallel with the individual perceived needs of the parent and student. This creates the environment in which teachers must respond with methods and approaches, and with understandings about the individuality, and hence the need for alternative methods of doing things in order for the classroom to function smoothly and efficiently.

Another frustrating aspect of teaching is the growing feeling of negativity toward education, and by association, educators. The authors are very proud that their oldest daughter Abby, who is currently a college sophomore, is majoring in elementary education at a Southern liberal arts institution. Unfortunately she has already had to struggle with comments from her college friends. Education as a profession is not viewed as a challenging course of study and this is illustrated by such comments as, "Oh, you're majoring in cutting or coloring." Other comments include, "Why do you want to do that? There's no money in it." Education as a profession does not appeal to many young people because it is a "fixed income" based on salary schedules established by state boards or state legislators. How sad that we must face such comments.

Another reality that often demotivates teachers is that we are often in conflict with our clientele. By this we mean that within our current structure of schools and classrooms, and within the current environment of education, there exists a strong incongruence between teacher-driven outcomes and student-desired outcomes. This topic of motivation, discussed at length in chapter 2, is a strong reality issue for the teachers. Here is an example. A middle school English teacher desires for her students to learn the deeper meaning of poetry; she explains to them that poetry can teach you more about yourself, that poetry is music to the soul, that poetry is life. The classroom is surrounded with poetry books and posters of some of the greatest poems ever written. The teacher works diligently on her lesson plans, she reads poems aloud with expression, and uses visuals where appropriate. She turns to her students and asks them what the poet is trying to say. She asks what the poet wants us to hear in his words. "Can you feel the urgency in the voice of the poet?" she asked. After the teacher uses the appropriate wait-time, finally one student very emphatically shouts, "No, I don't hear nothing!" That teacher goes home discouraged, and after much reflection, finally realizes that her goal was for her students to grasp the deeper meaning of poetry. Yet it seems that the student who shouted "No!" to the question of whether students can feel the urgency in the poet's voice, did not share the teacher's goal. What's ironic is that this same student might come back to see his middle school teacher when he is in high school and he'll proudly show her his report card. He's making a B in English. His favorite genre now is, you guessed it, poetry! This young man has the nerve to ask the teacher why she never taught poetry. Students aren't the only clientele with whom teachers are often in conflict. Others include parents, administrators, colleagues, friends, spouses, politicians, and the media, just to name a few.

It is this conflict that if it is not understood can become a major obstacle for teachers. The authors of this volume believe that conflict is a natural part of life, but the way in which it is dealt with separates successful people from unsuccessful ones. The examples we give of the realities of the teaching profession are not presented to discourage or demotivate those who currently teach or those who aspire to teach. Rather, we believe that an "eyes wide open" approach to the profession is needed in order to begin to make the changes necessary to our current state of affairs.

Also, it must be said that while frustrations do occur, they do not occur everywhere, every day, or all the time. Schools are still the best place for children. How teachers deal with these challenges becomes the real issue. So, having said all of this, what can be done, and more importantly, why do we continue?

Why Do We Continue?

We are definitely in a unique profession! Almost immediately, a doctor knows whether a surgery was successful; a lawyer knows success as soon as the judge rules, or the jury reads its verdict; and an architect sees success as a building is being built. Yet teachers only see snippets of the life of a child, and may have to wait for a long time to see the fruits that we sow and cultivate in the classroom.

Often we have found that many of the great teachers tend to focus on things other than immediate results. They relegate many of the successes to things that they learn from their students. While discussing these "learnings," we see embedded in their words the deep internalization into the compass points that direct us all to continue. The following reflection from a young teacher illustrates this point well. Read between the lines as you hear the passive voice of the teacher. What does she do and what will these actions mean for the future of her students?

It took me three trips to my car this year to load up all the Christmas presents I got from my kids. As I came back in from carrying the final load I looked at a friend and colleague of mine and said, "I think we may have just discovered the one benefit of overcrowded schools."

I have gotten a lot from being a teacher. What I have gotten, though, is immeasurably more than scented candles, lotion, coffee mugs, and baked cookies for the holidays. Allow me to share the real gift of teaching.

I remember the moment my fate was sealed and I decided to be a teacher. My freshman year in college I taught a kindergartner named Kristen how to write her name. I had been practicing with her for a while, and then one day she just sat down and did it. Kristen will probably never remember me or that moment. I, on the other hand, will remember thinking that I have just given something to a child that she will have and carry with her for the rest of her life. In that moment I was given a new direction, a new purpose.

For the rest of my college years and even when I first started teaching I thought I wanted to be a teacher because I had so much to give. I pictured myself sharing my knowledge, my talents, my faith, my love for learning, my ideals with some group of children who would embrace it wholeheartedly, go out and enlighten the world, then come back 20 years later and thank me. It turns out that my children have given me and taught me more than I have ever given to them.

John has taught me how important it is to show others how much I care for them. There are people in this world who are so devoid of love that one little word or hug means everything to them. John was not a popular boy and did not have a particularly good home life, either. John gave out 30 invitations to his birthday party. I was the only one who showed up. I will never forget the look on his face or the hug he gave me when he saw me walk through the door holding a balloon and candy for him. I miss the hugs he gave me. He always squeezed a little harder and held on a little longer than the other kids. Getting and giving that love is not something John gets at home or most other places. I thank John for showing me the impact of caring for others.

My kids have also given me a new understanding of what wonder is. I absolutely love to read because books can take me anywhere and let me be anyone. Even better than just reading, though, is reading to kids. I am amazed at their reactions and expressions to each new page and each twist in a story. Kids are the best audience because they are real, they are uninhibited. Part of me even loves when reading time comes to a close every day. I love that moment when I shut the book and the children all moan and beg for just one more page. My kids have given me a new appreciation for what it means to just let yourself get carried away—whether by a book, a person, a place, or even an emotion.

James has given me a new definition for the word "innocence." James is tiny for a third grader. He is dirty every day, he is hungry, he never has the supplies he needs, he has no support at home, and his few sets of clothes are ragged. Yet he is smart, he is beautiful, he is polite, he is kind-hearted. He is helpless. He is an eight-year-old who has had and will have to continue to raise himself without direction. He is that kid who melts a teacher's heart. He is that kid whose life can infuriate a teacher when you realize how much you want to help, but how little you can really do. He is just a kid at the mercy of a parent and a system that must not work well enough. He is the picture of innocence.

My kids have given me my eight-year-old self back. As adults, while we are in the company of other adults we tend to close down a bit and hold back. My kids have taught me how boring and fake that is. In my classroom, when the door is closed you never know what I may do—sing, dance, cry, laugh out loud, make ridiculous faces, or stand on my desk and tell stories. What other profession exists that lets you have recess every day? If businesspeople and politicians got to go down a slide, play on the swings, or kick a soccer ball around with a bunch of kids for 20 minutes every day, this world might be a better place. My kids have told me more times than I can count that I am crazy. I take that as a compliment. My kids have given me the opportunity to be Peter Pan every day, and I am a better person for it.

Hannah taught me about confidence. Hannah used to leave my room twice a day for extra help in reading and math. She used to always say things like, "I'm stupid," or "I can't do it." That year with her was such a struggle just to get her to believe in herself. After finalizing my grades, Hannah ended up getting an A in reading and a B+ in math for the fourth quarter. I was so proud of her and how hard she worked. I will never forget the look on her face when I showed her those final grades. I got to see her finally realize that she isn't stupid and she can do it. I got to see her believe in herself. This year Hannah still comes by my room to show off her tests when she makes an A. That look of confidence and pride is still on her face, and on mine as well.

Paul has taught me about love. As a young teacher, I've often been told that a teacher will have one special child who will always stay with them. For me that child is Paul. Paul has the saddest story I've ever heard. Paul has never gotten to be a kid, and probably never fully will. For most of the year he had so much anger in him that he would fly into a rage or just cry at the drop of a hat. I poured myself into that child like no one else. All he ever gave me in return was tears or telling me he hated me.

I have a whole notebook full of "hate mail" from him. I let him do it because I knew he didn't really mean it and because I knew I was the only person he could take his anger out on.

One day last year our guidance counselor came to my door while I was teaching and told me Paul's father killed himself. Paul was in my room at the time and did not know yet. Every time I looked at him my eyes filled up with tears. I wanted so badly to just hug him and protect him. Paul stayed out of school for a week after that. Every day of that school week I went to see him and hang out with him. The first time he let down his guard and hugged me was that week. He didn't say he hated me. He thanked me and told me he loved me. At the funeral Paul's sister told me that Paul said I was his hero. It's one year later now and a lot has changed in Paul's life, for better and for worse. Paul skips his recess often to come hang out with my new class and me. He talks now about how he, too, wants to be a third-grade teacher. Every time he pokes his head in the door to say hi or stops in for a visit I'm reminded of the power and responsibility of being a teacher. I'm reminded how important it is to love each child as much as I can for the brief time that I have with them, because I may never know what effect that love has on their lives.

John and Hannah and Paul and all those experiences and faces I see when I think about my time in the classroom have taught me more than I have ever learned sitting in an education class in college. They have given me a new love, a new passion, a new profession. They have let me have the gift of being their teacher.

(Sarah Tollick, second-year teacher)

Teaching is a synergy of relationships, and how we act or react sets the stage for these lessons to occur, for both student and teacher. It is within these relationships that the power of the teacher emerges, in the impact upon the child as well as the impact on society. Understanding this is sometimes delayed due to the lack of finality that we experience in our profession. Sarah continues to teach because she loves children, plain and simple. It is impossible for anyone to understand the joy of truly loving children and watching them learn unless you have the privilege of being a teacher.

Wendy Hawkins, mentor teacher at a small rural high-poverty school, continues to teach because she feels needed. She says, "Someone has entrusted me with these children for a reason. For a year of their life and the rest of mine they become my children. I care about them and I worry about them. I am intrigued by their thought processes and amazed at their resilience. I am not just a teacher. I am someone my children need in their lives, to teach them and hopefully make things better." Teachers don't continue to teach because of the perception floating out there that teaching is an easy job or because of the money. The rewards of teaching are far greater than the money or nonexistent summers off. Sometimes we continue to teach for that one child that we hope to reach.

I cannot believe how much I am enjoying the life of a teacher. Of course, the meetings and obligations aspect is not always the best, but nonetheless important. My kids have forced me to have a permanent smile on my face. Yes, they have also made me cry at times, but that's just because they make me realize how much I care about them. Sometimes they do something that just makes me realize how much they rely on and look up to me. I enjoy being a role model, but at the same time, it overwhelms me. I know that this is the role that God cut out for me a long time ago and I realize that fact every day, as things just seem to fall into place. I knew I was supposed to be a teacher, but the connection I have made with my kids has definitely put an exclamation mark on that belief. Thanks be! I have private moments of unexplainable tears as I think about the awesome role I have taken on.

It hit me for the first time when I was on the phone, returning a father's concerned phone call. He had called me at school because he was concerned about his son's behavior, learning abilities, and overall well-being. I was aware of the child's background, but the father went into detail about his son's past school experiences and how none of them had been good. He talked of the frustration this caused the child and parents. He told me how his son had been put in isolation a lot in the past because teachers were unable to deal with his behavior. (I quickly assured him that that has never and will never happen in my room.) Then, he got to the point of his call. He basically asked me if he and his wife should look into putting their son on Ritalin. Not only did a question of this magnitude hit me hard, but also how the father followed up his question really got me. He said to me "...because you spend more time with him during the day than I do." Okay, I admit, I was on the phone in the front office, in the presence of others, but I got a little teary-eyed. Before I began my response I told him that I was not a doctor of any kind and that I am not in any position to make a final decision. Then, I went on to tell him that I thought that Ritalin was an unnecessary step. I thought that it might ruin the child's self-esteem and that his behavior really wasn't a problem. I told the father that his son reminds me a lot of myself when I was that age. I often tell the child this as well and I think that really helps his confidence. Basically, I told the father that I was surprised by his call and that I did not have any problems with his son. Yes, I could see the tendencies, but nothing has disrupted my class or caused me to become concerned. The child is doing very well on assignments and behavior. I finished the half-hour conversation by telling the father that I am very proud of his son and that he should be, too. The father thanked me and told me that he felt a lot better. As soon as I hung up the phone I realized that I had just made some decisions for that child as if he were my son. I kind of just had to sit down for a little while and think. Since then, I have made a couple of positive contacts with that family just to update them on the behavior. The parents have said that this is the first time they have been happy with school and that they are actually looking forward to this year. I have seen the child become a better decision maker and a more productive student.

I have had many moments this year that have really forced me to reflect on my life. One mother thanked me for taking care of her daughter during the day. That deepened my awareness that I am not a schoolteacher, but a molder of lives (WOW!). I thank God for that awesome responsibility. No matter how stressful life gets or how forceful deadlines seem to be, when I am in my classroom I am at ease. If that is hard for anybody to believe I just tell them to come to my class and check it out. We truly have a caring, community atmosphere. It is evident in my kids' actions and especially in their smiles. I end each day with "hugs, high-fives, or hand shakes." A lot of my kids have turned it into "hugs, high-fives, and hand shakes." I have seen this help my kids open up more to affection. I receive many hugs throughout the day and am sure to give high-fives throughout the day as well. This has gone a long, long way in developing a caring, comfortable classroom environment. It is also my real "paycheck." We begin each day with a "share square" and I remind the kids that this is because I care more about what they do and think (their lives) than anything else. I let them know how much I care about them all the time!

(Colin Rork, first-year teacher)

Since ancient times, human beings have shared stories. Stories serve to bring laughter, to remind us of our past, to pass on our wisdom, and to bind us together. We share these stories with you in this chapter because they fuel our energy to continue. Henry Adams once said, "A teacher affects eternity; he can never tell where his influence stops" (Caruana, 1998). Teachers have current and postponed power. They are influencing our present and our future generations. However, teachers, too, are influenced and affected by their students. Another reason we continue to teach is for the ones who touch our hearts. The following reflection is from a first-year teacher who is entering the profession as a second career. Her reflection demonstrates the power that students have to touch our hearts.

Christmastime in an elementary school is a busy time for everyone, including the school librarian. The students are wild with excitement, the teachers are anxious to get through the day so they can take care of home and family Christmas traditions, and I am swamped with details to tend to before the year ends. Today is one week before Christmas break and I woke up with a headache. I anticipated seven classes in the media center for story time or research. The last thing I wanted to deal with was 20 four-year-olds for a library story hour. But they were coming so I got ready.

I have to admit that while I love conducting research classes with fourth and fifth grade students, four-year-olds however try my patience. I try to plan story times that will introduce the youngest children to good books and will entertain them. They love to tell me what is happening in their lives, so we always start our time together with a chance for the students to tell me things that are important to them. The students sit "criss-cross applesauce" on the floor and raise their hands, taking turns for the "privilege" of sharing a tidbit of excitement with their media specialist. Jackson raised his hand. Jackson is shorter than the other children in his class. He is a lovely little boy with a blond crew cut. He has a cute little speech impediment that causes him to say "k" for "t." His big blue eyes are framed by little round glasses. He is precious, and I smile when he starts speaking. Then I hear what he has to say.

"Know what?" he said, "My mommy moved to another house and I don't know why."

I asked him who took care of him and he said his daddy did.

Jackson continued, "But, know what? Mommy left when I was asleep and she didn't even kiss me and my brother good-bye."

It is Christmastime, and Jackson doesn't know how to have Christmas without Mommy. So he asked his librarian. I'm the information specialist, aren't I? The rest of the class period was conducted with tears in my eyes and a heavy heart. When I finished reading the story for the students, my assistant covered for me while I went for the tissues. Then she went for them when I repeated the conversation to her later.

Today I tried to be extra loving to all of the students, especially Jackson. Then I went to the guidance counselor and talked and cried with her. She was aware of the situation but did not realize Jackson was sad again. His mommy had moved out in September. Jackson is not being neglected; his daddy is doing a good job. Jackson's clothes look well tended. He is always clean when he comes to school. He brings his school materials daily, and he always has his library books. But Daddy is not Mommy, however much Daddy loves him. Jackson misses Mommy. He does not understand what was so important that she would leave in the night without kissing him good-bye. Jackson's teachers give him lots of love in the classroom. They are the kind of teachers who love all of their students and sharing that love is as important as teaching the ABCs, but they aren't Mommy, either.

Even in our relatively affluent school, we have children who come to school hungry, who have parents who are drug abusers (especially prescription drugs), and students who have slept only an hour or two the night before because no one would tuck them in. One child in our school has been removed from her home because her mother would not control her diet or follow the doctor's nutritional guidelines and the child was on her way to the same obesity that has bound her mother to a wheelchair. Our school nurse tells us that the number one reason children miss school is because of dental health problems. I see the little children with rotten teeth and I wonder, "How can anyone concentrate on school when they have a toothache?"

It breaks my heart. My two sons have been given every advantage and all the love and support their father and I can pour into their lives. Yet, they still occasionally choose not to do homework or to do less than their best. What possible chance do some of our elementary children have to succeed in school when their parents have abandoned their role and the students are hungry, tired, unloved, and unsupported? We have students whose parents have told teachers that they are not interested in hearing about homework anymore. Some students have missed as many as 20 to 30 days already, and we are only halfway through the school year.

How much love can one teacher offer, and will it ever be enough? My students come to me and I think of them as little vessels, ready to be filled with the knowledge I have planned so carefully to impart. Today it became obvious to me that many of our students' vessels are already full with what takes place at home. How can four-year-old Jackson focus on learning his spatial relationships or colors when he is worried about how to have Christmas without Mommy? How can teachers expect our students to do their homework when no one at home cares if it is done or not? What value will be placed on education when parents don't care enough to put their little children to bed on time? And when Mommy or Daddy are faced with problems that would leave me curled on my couch in a fetal position humming "You Are My Sunshine," how can I expect them to be the ideal parent?

In my heart, I know that good teachers make a difference in their students' lives. I have heard the testimonies of adults who were inspired by the love and kindness shown them by their teachers. I have seen students' faces light up because of a kind word or gentle touch from me in the library. Sometimes, however, the task seems enormous. There are so many of them to love, so many to inspire, so many to encourage, so many Jacksons.

My headache never did go away, and I added heartache to it. Today I learned it is so important for me to be kind and loving, all of the time. I learned I must remember that children come to my library full of things over which I have no control and they cannot change. I learned I cannot be Mommy to all of them, but I can be a loving adult in their lives. I just hope it is enough, but I fear it cannot be.

(Monique German, second career, first-year teacher [media specialist])

We continue to teach because it is fun! We teach because each day is a new day and each day holds hundreds of possibilities. Sure, we have our lesson plans but we never really know what will happen or how our students will react to the day's activities. There is excitement and laughter in the classroom. Humor, indeed, abounds in classrooms and schools. Much of the time, the opportunities for it to occur naturally crop up in places other than the classroom and at times that are not designed to be instructional. These may be in the hallways, the office, or perhaps more often in the cafeteria at lunchtime. The following is a reflection of a conversation shared by Laurie Ingram during the first week of her senior internship.

- At lunchtime the kids got fortune cookies, and Austin's fortune was "You are a true romantic." He asked me what romantic meant, and I thought quickly and said, "Um, it means you like happy endings and for everything to work out nicely." And Austin, speaking like a true male, said, "I work out! My daddy and I go to the gym!" Ten years from now, all the girls in his class are going to be vying for his attention, and poor Austin thinks he's a "true romantic" because he goes to the gym.

- Lunchtime conversation:
  Child 1: "How old are you?"
  Miss Ingram: "Twenty-one."
  Child 2: "Does that mean you're a teenager?"
  Child 3: "No! It means she's married!"

- Lunchtime conversation another day:
  Autumn: "Are you a kid or a grown-up?"
  Laurie: (ponders to herself—I never know the answer to that question!)
  "I think definitely...a grown-up."
  Autumn: "But how can you be a grown-up if you're so fun?"

- Austin: "When you were little, how many whoopins did you get a week?"
  Laurie: "Gee, Austin, I think hardly any...I was a very well-behaved little girl."
  Austin: (studying Laurie curiously, then breaking into a huge grin) "Naaaah!"

The power of the teacher shown in the comments in these situations is merely in the fact that the conversations occurred to begin with. The students will long remember Miss Ingram, not because of what she said but because she listened, responded, and shared some of herself with them. What a wonderful thought! Teaching and learning can occur in places other than within the four walls of the classroom.

At the end of her first year of teaching, Michelle Johnson, a first-year teacher, shares her thoughts.

> I wanted to become a teacher because I adore children and I wanted to inspire young minds. Nearing the end of my first year of teaching, I realize that teachers are devoted people who must be passionate about their careers. I now understand the trials, the laughs, the stresses, the heartbreaks, the pleasures, and the frustrations. Teachers do inspire children. However, during my first year, I learned an even more valuable and motivating lesson. Each child in my classroom needs, cares, motivates, humors, challenges, fascinates, and pleases me. With all that their young and eager minds have to offer, how couldn't I be inspired and why wouldn't I want to continue in this career that can give so much? Teachers may be given the credit for being the ones to inspire, but after spending day after day with my first group of students, I see that children inspire teachers.

How do we sum this up? We believe that we continue to teach because of a set of beliefs that drive us to do so. Simply put, there is worth and dignity to be found in all people, especially children, and it is the teacher's job to discover each child's potential and unlock it. Without the teacher as the key, the gifts remain undiscovered and the child, as well as his or her future, is diminished. This is why we continue.

How Can We Continue?

This question is one that our profession must face, and do so quickly. If we look at what lies ahead in today's system of public education, we readily see that most of the obstacles that challenge us the most have been evident for many years. We have enumerated them throughout this text and believe that they are led by the sweep of high-stakes testing as a single measure of school accountability and effectiveness. Is it possible to continue teaching? Yes, we believe it is, and the solution resides first and foremost with the power that is within ourselves.

If teaching exudes so much power, then how do we translate that power to an effective solution for the ills that the system now has?

We believe that teachers must exert themselves as leaders in the profession and serve as positive change agents for the profession. How can this happen without civil disobedience? The authors of this volume believe that it can as long as the organization that we call education will allow it. First let's look at the components that we believe exist in effective school systems and schools.

Generally, people tend to look at organizations in a holistic manner. In other words, people see the school system as reigning supreme and the components such as schools and classrooms simply following suit to the direction that emanates from above. Instead, we believe that school systems are more individual, with each division operating as a separate microcosm of the larger whole. Along with this, we also believe that the most effective subsystems operate under a conceptual power structure where power resides in three basic positions—the superintendent, the principal, and the teacher. Each subsystem extends the power structure. By this we mean that the system (superintendent) involves the principals in shared decision making, the school (principal) involves the teachers in decision making, and most importantly, the classroom (teacher) involves the students in decision making. This is simply the vision of the organization that permeates its culture.

Successful school systems possess an effective leadership team that is engineered by the superintendent, just as successful schools have the same organization that is led by the principal with classrooms that are led by effective teachers. It is, simply put, the direction of the organization. This vision must be shared and viewed as the engine for the organization and is developed through a complex cultured process. While direction of the organization must be top-down, the vision is top-down, bottom up, and side to side. It is this multidirectional concept and full empowerment of all stakeholders that allows the vision to be truly shared.

Once the vision is conceived and internalized into the organizational culture successful school systems appear to have the capacity for the system to have the "know-how" to achieve the mission. This "I can do it" attitude is the direct result of the continuous assessment of the instructional readiness of the organization as well as the realistic knowledge of the resource limitations of the system. It is this combination of expertise and resource availability that allows for the exploration of problems of the organization and the identification of potential solutions within the context of attainable outcomes.

Further, school systems that are successful experience system wide feelings of support from key leadership. In other words, the superintendent, the principal, and the teacher are truly supportive, caring, nurturing, and helping. This feeling or belief is a direct result of the established inclusive nature of the organization. The fuel for this inclusion is the open line of communication that exists at *all* levels of the system.

Additionally, successful organizations understand their past as a key to their future. This means that the culture and history of the system are analyzed and appreciated. This concept is paramount to the success of the system. How can you know where you are going if you don't understand where you have been? So often systems react in knee-jerk fashion without reflection to see whether or not commonalities and connections exist between current situations and past realities. This provides a platform for learning and building on past practices and experiences and provides a fruitful starting point for progress. Knowing who you are and where you have been is critical to establishing a cohesive environment for changes. It is at this point that change becomes less painful and threatening due to the comfort from understanding and appreciating school culture and history. These major factors serve as a compass to guide organizations toward success, stability, and continued progress in the continuing struggle to focus on the overall mission of all school districts—the success of its students. It is the understanding of these intricate relationships that allow this to efficiently occur.

Let's take a minute to look back at the realities of teaching mentioned earlier in this chapter. The first issue is the fact that a teacher's job is never, ever finished. However, with time (and patience) we learn to cope with the feeling of never being finished. We learn that it is important to keep lists, to prioritize items as to what must be accomplished today and what can wait. We learn to manage our time better and we learn to delegate. Greg had the opportunity to attend a one-day workshop on time management. The leader of the workshop was speaking to a group of school administrators and, to drive home a point, used the following illustration.

> As he stood in front of the group of high-powered overachievers, he said, "Okay, time for a quiz." Then he pulled out a one-gallon, wide-mouthed mason jar and set it on the table in front of him. Then he produced about a dozen fist-sized rocks and carefully placed them, one at a time, into the jar. When the jar was filled to the top and no more rocks would fit inside, he asked, "Is this jar full?"
>
> Everyone in the class said, "Yes." Then he said, "Really?" He reached under the table and pulled out a bucket of gravel. Then he dumped some gravel in and shook the jar, causing pieces of gravel to work themselves down into the space between the big rocks. Then he asked the group once more, "Is the jar full?" By this time the class was on to him. "Probably not," one of them answered. "Good!" he replied. He reached under the table and brought out a bucket of sand. He dumped the sand in the jar and

it went into all of the spaces left between the rocks and the gravel. Once more he asked the question, "Is this jar full?" "No!" the class shouted. Once again he said, "Good."

Then he grabbed a pitcher of water and began to pour it in until the jar was filled to the brim. Then he looked at the class and asked, "What is the point of this illustration?"

One eager beaver raised his hand and said, "The point is, no matter how full your schedule is, if you try really hard you can always fit some more things in it!" "No," the speaker replied. "That's not the point. The truth this illustration teaches us is: If you don't put the big rocks in first, you'll never get them in at all. What are the big rocks in your life? Your children? Loved ones? Your education? Your dreams? A worthy cause? Teaching or mentoring others? Doing things that you love? Time for yourself? Your health? Your significant other? Remember to put these big rocks in first or you'll never fit them all in. If you sweat the little stuff (the gravel, the sand), then you'll fill your life with little things you worry about that don't really matter, and you'll never have the real quality time you need to spend on the big, important stuff (the big rocks). So, tonight, or in the morning, when you are reflecting on this short story, ask yourself this question: What are the big rocks in my life? Place those in your jar first."

This story illustrates the point that it is necessary to identify the important things. Every teacher is different when it comes to managing his or her day. Effective teachers find ways to manage the paperwork, lesson plans, communicating with parents, and fulfilling professional obligations. Look for ways to have others help in the tasks. Can older students assist with some of the daily tasks? Students enjoy the power of assisting teachers! Are there tutors available? What about parents helping you to gather materials or run off papers? Celebrate items that are marked off the endless list and know that each day is a new day!

The second reality of teaching is having alternative methods of doing things. Teaching is a people-oriented business and certainly we can't have exact solutions to situations that arise each day in the classroom. In fact, the authors of this text believe that we should not strive for sameness. This challenge of alternative methods should be our hidden ammunition against meeting the diverse needs of the students in our classes. Experience is always the best teacher regarding how to handle the day-to-day operations of a classroom; however, we must not stop there in our search for the best way to "do school." As discussed in the previous chapter, we must take charge of our own professional development. We need to continue to take university courses, upgrade our teaching certificate, hold memberships in professional organizations, and attend professional conferences where our interaction and dialogue with other colleagues is critical to our growth. We must retool and upgrade our knowledge and skills by reading professional books and periodicals.

Teachers who read professional articles and search the Internet for new methods are more equipped to make changes in their classes.

The next reality of teaching is the growing state of public negativity toward teaching and teachers. We believe that this attitude neither occurred overnight nor will it change quickly. There must be a resurgence of pride within our own profession. We can get this pride by exerting leadership. The means to attaining this pride include professional organizations, the use of action research, and even an active role in the political arena. We must change ourselves so that we may change our classrooms. Only then will the perception of our profession follow suit.

The last reality of teaching discussed in this book involves conflict with our clientele. First, we must know what groups compromise the category "clientele." This knowledge allows us to be proactive. Obviously, we know that children are our primary clients, but too often we find ourselves catering to the other groups to the detriment of our primary customers. This plays itself out in politically correct curriculum choices, methodologies, and pedagogy. We sometimes do this because the groups who demand this speak with a louder voice. This can be described as the "squeaky wheel getting more of the grease." The authors of this text believe that if we do more with our primary clients (students), the squeaking will stop. So what do we do? First, remember that nobody goes into this profession to tell people what to do and to make them do it every day. We must continue to evaluate ourselves and our approaches using what we know about student development and motivation. We must create classrooms where students own most of their learning. People tend to value what they create. This alone will reduce much of the conflict. These principles of ownership, choice, and participation reflect the characteristics of the democratic classroom. We should strive for these things and we believe the other audiences will follow suit to re-create the respect, confidence, and support of teachers and the institution of American education. Certainly, there are many obstacles that exist that must be negotiated, but we believe that teachers have the ability to focus on the end result and to do what is necessary to meet the desired outcomes.

Conclusion

In this chapter, we have presented information that we believe to be key in understanding the power of this profession. To some, these words will "inspire"; to others, they will cause them to "perspire"; and to a few others, they will cause a desire to "retire" from teaching. If you find yourself in the first category, you are set to meet the challenges that await us. You teach with both your head and your heart, respect the dignity of all students, as well as respect the content of the subject that you teach. You believe that for your students to learn, they must first learn to lead. By that we mean, that to inspire students we must instill within them the desire to take ownership in their learning and thus become lifelong learners. A master can tell what he expects of you, a teacher awakens your own expectations.

If you are in the middle, we believe that you must begin now to plan for your own future. Teaching is difficult yet it is rewarding. These are not necessarily polarized events, but they do intersperse and many times come in waves of varying degrees. This environment requires a willingness to use diagnostic ability and to act on that diagnosis even to the point of leaving one's comfort zone. Teaching is not for everyone, but the children deserve only the best that we have to offer. Finally, if you find yourself in the last group, wanting to retire, now is the time to leave!

Teaching is not for the faint hearted. It requires a commitment unlike no other profession. Let's illustrate the depth of that commitment with the following tale. Once upon a time there was a very happy barnyard with a very attentive farmer. The animals were all well fed and they were housed in comfortable conditions. One morning the animals were talking about how good their lives were and the suggestion was made to do something to reward the farmer for his kindness to them. After some discussion, it was determined that they would give him a special breakfast. The cow would provide a nice glass of fresh milk, the chicken two large eggs, and the pig the bacon. When the special day arrived, the trio gathered in the barnyard. The cow had the milk, the chicken had the eggs, but the pig had nothing. Immediately the cow and the chicken began to chastise the selfish pig. "We all agreed to this," they said. The pig dejectedly looked down and said, "Listen, for you this breakfast means a contribution; for me it's a commitment!"

We must move beyond just contributing to our profession and make a real commitment. That is what it will take to capitalize on the true power of the profession.

In the early 1990s we had the opportunity to hear a speech by the 1987 United States Teacher of the Year, Guy Doud. In his presentation he related his visit to the Oval Office to meet then president, Ronald Reagan. In his remembrance of that meeting, he shared a poem that President Reagan read to him. It was a poem written by Clark Mollenhoff. We believe the poem sums up this chapter much better than we can. It is our hope that all teachers will strive to live by these words.

Teachers

You are the molders of their dreams.

The gods who build or crush their young beliefs of right or wrong.

You are the spark that sets aflame the poet's hand or lights the flame in
  some great singer's song.

You are the gods of young—the very young.

You are the guardian of a million dreams.

Your every smile or frown can heal or pierce a heart.

Yours are one hundred lives—one thousand lives

Yours is the pride of loving them, the sorrow too.

Your patient work, your touch, makes the god of hope that fills their
  souls with dreams, and makes those dreams come true.

CONCLUSION

Education is both a science and an art. The science of education uses the teacher's mind in matters such as planning, organizational skills, schedules, administration, and designing curriculum. Teachers need to keep the material fresh and interesting each time it is presented. Even though they've taught the subject a thousand times before, we must remember it is the first time for the student. As a teacher, you have tremendous influence and power over the students; you can mold an appreciation for life, depending on your approach. Creating a learning environment filled with trust, creativity, empowerment, and collaboration enhances the learning process, and motivates and energizes students. It is proven that humor helps students to retain information better, so we should make humor an integral part of the curriculum rather than using it only after completing serious work.

The art of education involves the heart, listening to students, and most importantly caring about them. Teaching from the heart cannot be reduced to technique; it comes from identity and integrity. Good teachers weave themselves, their students, and their subjects into one. Teachers make demands, offer support and encouragement, set goals and give praise when goals are reached. A teacher's main job is to help students fall in love with learning. Students need to learn to appreciate their own individuality and discover common ground as well. When teaching goes hand-in-hand with intellect, emotion, and spirit, it enhances learning. Great teachers capitalize on all opportunities to reach the reachable as well as the unreachable, the motivated as well as the unmotivated, the loved as well as the unloved. Ultimately, the goal for the teacher is to teach students how to develop their own "internal teacher" so that their communication and motivation doesn't leave when the teacher is gone.

School is an essential support system for any culture. We must avoid a system that supports social engineering condemning most people to be subordinate stones in a pyramid that narrows to a control point as it ascends. The future insists that we make a choice at the crossroads that we are approaching. In more traveled roads, school is a place where students are sentenced to a 12-year jail term. We must draw upon all the characteristics of our successful colleagues and those who have gone before to make the correct choice upon our arrival at this intersection. We need to understand that we indeed shape the lives of our students to a large degree.

When the day is done, always remember that the single most important link in the chain to the future is the teacher. Troubled times only make the ultimate destination in the journey all the more satisfying.

REFERENCES

Albert, L. (1989). *A teacher's guide to cooperative discipline: How to manage your classroom and self-esteem.* Circle Pines, MN: American Guidance Service.

Anderson, C. (1985). The Investigation of School Climate. *Research on Exemplary Schools,* edited by G. R. Austin and H. Garber. Orlando, FL: Academic Press, 97–126.

Atkinson, K. (1973, [Feb. 25, 2003]). Cipher in the snow. *Classroom Support Services.* Available: www.css.washington.edu/emc/titles.

Barth, R., (1990). *Improving schools from within.* San Francisco: Jossey-Bass.

Boreen, J. (2000). *Mentoring beginning teachers.* York, ME: Stenhouse.

Brooks, S., Freiburger, S., & Grotheer, D. (1998). *Improving elementary student engagement in the learning process through integrated thematic instruction.* Unpublished master's thesis, Saint Xavier University, Chicago, Ill.

Brophy, J. (1986, April). *Socializing students' motivation to learn.* Paper presented at the annual meeting of the American Educational Research Association, San Francisco.

Cahn, D. (1986). Perceived understanding, supervisor-subordinate communication, and organizational effectiveness. *Communication Studies,* 37, 19–26.

Canter, L., & Canter, M. (1992). *Assertive discipline.* Santa Monica, CA: Lee Canter Associates.

Caruana, V. (1998). *Apples and chalkdust: Inspirational stories and encouragement for teachers.* Tulsa, OK: Honor Books.

Covey, S. (1998). *Seven habits of highly effective people.* New York: Simon & Schuster.

Covington, M. V., & Beery, R. (1976). *Self-worth and school learning.* New York: Holt, Rinehart & Winston.

Culham, R. (2003). *6 + 1 Traits of Writing.* New York: Scholastic, Inc.

Deal, T., & Peterson, K. (1998). *Shaping school culture: The heart of leadership.* San Francisco: Jossey-Bass.

Dev, P. (1997). Intrinsic motivation and academic achievement: What does their relationship imply for the classroom teacher? *Remedial and Special Education,* 18(1), 12–19.

Dewey, J. (1910). *How we think.* Boston: D. C. Heath.

———. (1994). Democracy *and education.* Shelburne, VT.: Resource Center for Redesigning Education. (Original work published 1916.)

Doyle, W. (1983). Academic work. Review of educational research, 53, 159–199.

———. (1986). *Classroom organization and management.* New York: Macmillan.

Feather, N. (1982). Expectations and actions. Hillsdale, NJ: Erlbaum.

Fielstein, L., & Phelps, P. (2001). Introduction to teaching: Rewards and realities. Stanford, CT: Wadsworth.

Galloway, C. (1976). *Silent language in the classroom.* (Report no. 130 337). East Lansing, MI: National Center for Research on Teacher Learning. ERIC Document Reproduction Service.

Gallup, A. (1984). The Gallup poll of teachers' attitudes toward the public schools. *Phi Delta Kappan,* 66, 97–101.

————. (1987 [February 26, 2003]). Gallup Opinion Polls: Public Education and K-12 Teacher Members. National Education Association Research Center. Available: www.nes.org./he/research/html

Gardner, H. (1995). Reflections on multi-intelligences. *Phi Delta Kappan*, 77(3), 300–309.

Ginott, H. (1972). *Teacher and child: A book for parents and teachers.* New York: Macmillan.

Glasser, W. (1988). On students' needs and team learning: A conversation with William Glasser. *Educational Leadership*, 45, 38–45.

————. (1989). *Discipline without tears.* New York: Harper & Row.

————. (1990). *The quality schools: Managing students without coercion.* New York: Harper & Row.

Goodlad, J. (1984). *A place called school.* New York: McGraw-Hill.

————. (1990). *Teachers for our nation's schools.* San Francisco: Jossey-Bass.

Gregorian, V. (2001, July 6). How to train and retrain teachers. *The New York Times*, B15.

Hunter, M. (1995). *Mastery teaching.* Thousand Oaks, CA: Corwin Press.

Jackson, A., & Davis, K. (2000). *Turning points 2000: Educating adolescents in the 21st century.* Boston, MA: Center for Collaborative Education.

Jensen, R., & Kiley, T. (2000). *Teaching, leading, and learning: Becoming caring professionals.* Boston: Houghton Mifflin.

John-Steiner, V. (1997). *Notebooks of the mind: Explorations of thinking.* New York: Oxford University Press.

Jones, V. (1980). *Adolescents with behavior problems: Strategies for teaching, counseling, and parent involvement.* Boston: Allyn & Bacon.

Jones, V., & Jones, L. (1998). *Comprehensive classroom management: Creating communities of support and solving problems.* Boston: Allyn & Bacon.

Keefe, J. W., & Jenkins, J. M. (1997). *Instruction and the learning environment.* Larchmont, NY: Eye on Education.

Kincheloe, J. (1995). *Toil and Trouble.* New York: Peter Lang.

Kincheloe, J., Slattery, P., & Steinberg, S. (2000). *Contextualizing teaching.* New York: Longman.

Kohl, H. (1999[February 26, 2003]). U.S. Senate Hearing. Crisis in math and science education. Washington, D.C. Available: www.teachon.com/zizi/quotes

Kohn, A. (1993). *Punishment by rewards: The trouble with gold stars, incentive plans, A's, praise, and other bribes.* Boston: Houghton Mifflin.

Kounin, J. (1970). *Discipline and group management in classrooms.* New York: Holt, Rinehart, & Winston.

Lappan, G., & Ferrini-Mundy, J. (1993, May). Knowing and Doing Mathematics: A New Vision for Middle Grade Students. *The Elementary School Journal*, 93(5), 625–641.

Latinos in school: Some facts and findings. (2001). (ERIC Digest No.162). East Lansing, MI: National Center for Research on Teacher Learning. (ERIC Document Reproduction Service No. ED 449 288.)

Lumsden, L. (1994). Student motivation to learn. (ERIC Digest No. 92). Eugene, OR: ERIC Clearinghouse on Educational Management. (ERIC Document Reproduction Service No. ED 370 200.)

Mauer, M., & Zimmerman, E. (2000, January). Mentoring new teachers. *Principal*, 79, 26–28.

McCroskey, J. (1992). *An introduction to communication in the classroom.* Edina, MN: Burgess International Group.

Montano-Harmon, M. (1991, May). Discourse features of written Mexican Spanish: Current research in contrastive rhetoric and its implications. *Hispania*, 74 (2), 417–425.

Morse, W. (1994). Self-concept in the school setting. *Childhood Education*, 41, 195–198.

National Commission on Teaching and America's Future. (1996). What matters most: Teaching for America's future. New York: Author.

Noguera, P. (1995). Preventing and producing violence: A critical analysis of responses to school violence. *Harvard Educational Review,* 65, 189–212.

Palmer, P. (1998). *The courage to teach.* San Francisco: Jossey-Bass.

Patton, M. (1980). Qualitative evaluation methods. Beverly Hills, CA: Sage Publications.

Payne, R. (2001). *A framework for understanding poverty.* Highlands, TX: Aha! Process, Inc.

Raffini, J. (1993). *Winners without losers: Structures and strategies for increasing student motivation to learn.* Boston: Allyn & Bacon.

Ramsey, S. (1979). Nonverbal behavior: An intercultural perspective. In M. K. Asante, E. Newmark, & C. A. Blake (Eds.). *Handbook of intercultural communication* (pp. 105–143) Beverly Hills, CA: Sage.

Robinson, R. (1995). Affinitive communication behaviors: A comparative analysis of the interrelationships among teacher nonverbal immediacy, responsiveness, and verbal receptivity on the prediction of student learning. Paper presented at the annual convention of the International Communication Association, Albuquerque, NM.

Rogers, D., & Webb, J. (1991). The ethic of caring in teacher education. *Journal of Teacher Education,* 42, 173–181.

Rosenthal, R., & Jacobson, L. (1968). *Pygmalion in the classroom: Teacher expectation and pupils' intellectual development.* New York: Holt, Rinehart, & Winston.

Scheflen, A. (1972). On communicational processes. In A. Wolfgang (Ed.), *Nonverbal behavior: Applications and cultural implications.* New York: Academic Press.

Schon, D. (1983). *The reflective practitioner: How professionals think in action.* San Francisco: Jossey-Bass.

Sergiovanni, T. (1994). *Building community in schools.* San Francisco: Jossey-Bass.

Skinner, E., & Belmont, M. (1991). A longitudinal study of motivation in school: Reciprocal effects of teacher behavior and student engagement. Unpublished manuscript, University of Rochester, Rochester, New York.

Spady, W. (1999). *Paradigm lost: Reclaiming America's educational future.* Arlington, VA: American Association of School Administrators.

Sternberg, R., & Lubart, T. (1995). *Defying the crowd: Cultivating creativity in a culture of conformity.* New York: Free Press.

Stipec, D. (1988). *Motivation to learn: From theory to practice.* Englewood Cliffs, NJ: Prentice-Hall.

Wagar, W. (1963). *The city of man, prophecies of a modern civilization in twentieth century thought.* Boston: Houghton Mifflin.

Wells, A. (1989). *Middle school education: The critical link in dropout prevention.* (Report no. 56). New York: ERIC Clearinghouse on Urban Education.

Wiggins, G. & McTighe, J. (1998). *Understanding by design.* Alexandria, VA: ASCD.

Wong, H., & Wong, R. (1995). *The first days of school: How to be an effective teacher.* Mountain View, CA: Harry Wong Publications.

extreme teaching
rigorous texts for troubled times

Joe L. Kincheloe and Danny Weil
General Editors

Books in this series will provide practical ideas on classroom practice for teachers and teacher educators that are grounded in a profound understanding of the social, cultural, political, economic, historical, philosophical, and psychological contexts of education as well as in a keen sense of educational purpose. Within these contextual concerns contributors will address the ferment, uncertainty, and confusion that characterize the troubles of contemporary education. The series will focus specifically on the act of teaching. While the topics addressed may vary, EXtreme Teaching is ultimately a book series that addresses new, rigorous, and contextually informed modes of classroom practice. Authors will bring together a commitment to educational and social justice with a profound understanding of a rearticulation of what constitutes compelling scholarship. The series is based on the insight that the future of progressive educational reform rests at the intersection of socio-educational justice and scholarly rigor. Authors will present their conceptions of this rigorous new pedagogical frontier in an accessible manner that avoids the esoteric language of an "in group." In this context, the series editors will make use of their pedagogical expertise to introduce pedagogical ideas to student, teacher, and professional audiences. In this process, they will explain what they consider the basic concepts of a field of study, developing their own interpretive insights about the domain and how it should develop in the future. Very few progressive texts exist to introduce individuals to rigorous and complex conceptions of pedagogical practice: thus, authors will be expected to use their contextualized interpretive imaginations to introduce readers to a creative and progressive view of pedagogy in the field being analyzed.

For additional information about this series or for the submission of manuscripts, please contact:

Joe L. Kincheloe & Danny Weil
c/o Peter Lang Publishing, Inc.
275 Seventh Avenue, 28th floor
New York, New York 10001

To order other books in this series, please contact our Customer Service Department:
(800) 770-LANG (within the U.S.)
(212) 647-7706 (outside the U.S.)
(212) 647-7707 FAX

Or browse online by series at *www.peterlangusa.com*